BREAKING THROUGH,

SELLING OUT,

DROPPING DEAD

Breaking Through, Selling Out, Dropping Dead

WILLIAM S. BAYER

The Macmillan Company
New York, New York

The Macmillan Company
866 Third Avenue, New York, N.Y. 10022

Library of Congress Catalog Card Number: 78–160079

First Printing

Printed in the United States of America

CONTENTS

E

F

G

H

I

J

L

M

N

P

BREAKING THROUGH,

SELLING OUT,

DROPPING DEAD

INTRODUCTION

This book is not about the aesthetics of the cinema, nor is it meant to be a handbook of motion-picture-production techniques. Rather it is a collection of random, subjective, and often idiosyncratic notes about filmmaking—attitudes, facts, speculations, and suggestions, many of which may antagonize the reader and some of which may give him thought.

It is intended for and addressed to the young filmmaker who is faced with enormous problems of career development; who is coming close to embarking upon a first feature; who is exploring ways of financing, organizing, and selling an independent picture; and who is looking for a way to work within that structure called "the film industry." The reader is frequently addressed as "you," and there are certain things assumed about this "you" that it is best to state at the onset.

The first assumption is that you want to work with the "big screen." The "big screen" is not found in school auditoriums or at short-film-subject festivals or in the screening rooms of museums, and it does not have to do with television, or industrial shorts, or even, with rare exceptions, documentaries. The "big screen" is the huge and dominating screen of the movie theatre. This book, then, is intended for those who want to make feature films.

The second assumption is that you are not one of those people who wander around saying, very casually, "In a few years I'd like to try a feature." Rather it is supposed that you want to make features more than anything else, that you are totally committed to feature films as a form of self-expression, and that you are prepared to do whatever is necessary to make them— short of compromising your moral and artistic standards.

The third assumption is that whether you like the system or despise it, you are aware that if you want to make features, you must somehow find a way of working within the existing structure. You are also aware that the best way of doing this is to understand that structure so thoroughly that you can fight it on its own terms and succeed in spite of it. The corollary of this, of course, is that changing the system is a life's work, and the man who wants to combine revolutionary impulses with filmmaking (a perfectly admirable decision) should realize that he is renouncing film as a means of creating art.

The fourth and final assumption is that you are an artist, that you have talent, and that you also have something to say. The problem for you, then, is how to transfer the fantasy you harbor in your mind onto the screen where it can be communicated to other people.

Much of what is said here is unpleasant. It is not very inspiring to read or to write about the stealing that is done by distributors and exhibitors, competition, ruthlessness, power, and a thousand other loathsome subjects. I decided to write about these matters because in talking with film students over the last couple of years I have observed a naiveté which no one else has bothered to set right.

Frankly, my experiences with film students have been depressing. I have found many lost souls with grand fantasies of being directors: sensitive, gentle, and often Christlike kids who seem to feel that they can find themselves with film. I think the universities and the media have done a great disservice by creating and perpetuating the illusion that "things are opening up" and "the young filmmaker is being searched out and sought after."

If there is a central thesis to these notes it is that the would-be filmmaker has an enormous fight ahead of him, and that that lost look of ennui one finds in so many film students is part of a general sickness that has come over the land: the belief that everyone has within himself the vision and talent to create art, and that film, being the art of the time, is as good a place to start as any.

I don't think this is true. I think film is the most demanding and frustrating art form ever devised, and that the filmmaker's need for money, and the qualities of stamina, leadership, and ability to collaborate (which are so rarely combined with talent) make it a perilous profession in which only a few can survive.

There is much talk these days about a revolution in consciousness: a rejection of competitiveness, "making it," and success. There are, in addition to these progressive changes in consciousness, some other ideas which I consider regressive: a scorn of elitism in the arts, and a general downgrading of excellence. In any event, despite certain visible inroads in other areas, the consciousness revolution has not begun to touch the film industry. It is naive for a filmmaker to think that the counter-culture is going to devise a way of making and distributing pictures that will make film accessible to everyone as a means of self-expression. Eventually we can hope that a viable alternative to the practices of the industry will be discovered. Some method must be found for the filmmaker who wants to work in an intimate way, and who cannot bear to spend most of his time hustling money. There must also be found a means of access to the theatrical screen, so long denied those whose work is not conventionally commercial. It is my suspicion that these changes will not come about because of any change in consciousness, or on account of a technological breakthrough (i.e., video cassettes), but will only occur when the people who make films get themselves together, make a stand, and take back the domination of their profession from the businessmen who now control it. That revolution, however, is a long way off, and the problems of the young filmmaker today cannot be solved by wishful thinking. Thus this book: a collection of notes on these problems, some definitions of attitudes one may take toward them, and some ideas on film production thrown in for good measure.

Academy Awards

The vast gulf that separates the filmmaking-industrial complex and the aspirant filmmaker is nowhere better illustrated than in the annual comic-operetta known as The Awards Ceremonies of the American Academy of Motion Picture Arts and Sciences. Everything about this event seems calculated to make the young filmmaker laugh, sneer, and squirm with anxiety.

There is, first of all, the characteristic cynicism of the industry. A man from Price Waterhouse is trotted out to confirm that the balloting has been honest and that the names of the winners have been held in strict confidence. Meantime the trade papers have been clamoring about various forms of bloc-voting and politicking indulged in by the studios, including the wining and dining of Academy members and other, less subtle, efforts to obtain a coveted Oscar for a picture that needs a boost at the box office.

Television coverage is thorough and insures that we see every moment of the event: tight closeups of the nominees sweating it out in dinner jackets and evening gowns, biting their nails as the tension builds; announcements by glamorous actors and actresses whose entrances from separate sides of the stage seem choreographed for a high-school graduation; rushes forward and emotional acceptance speeches; and, finally, winners so dazed by the certainty that their prices have just doubled for their next picture becoming temporarily confused and being led off stage by the stern hand of Bob Hope.

Beneath the farce there is a distressing truth: the Oscar is still a persuasive mark of excellence to segments of the general public, and *the nominees and winners represent what the establishment of the industry thinks is good.*

The young filmmaker should watch this event and scrutinize it closely. It may seem to him like something from another planet, but he should remember that this "Academy" is an elite who will decide whether or not he is going to make pictures. It is a chilling thought.

Actors

Many young filmmakers know a great deal about cameras and editing and sound, and very little about actors. Part of the reason is that the first films they make are usually documentaries, and the first problem they face is achieving mastery over the technical aspects of film. There is also a fascination with the intricate mechanisms of equipment and the sensuality of working with one's hands that is very much a part of the pleasure of making pictures. This tendency to exalt the technical is unfortunate because actors are more important tools than cameras, tape recorders, and editing machines, and their mechanisms are more intricate, more sensitive, and of infinitely greater interest. The neglect of the actor in film schools is a real problem, and it shows in many of the pictures of young filmmakers.

One must remember that in film, which is a humanistic art, the actor is indispensable. Brilliant cinematography cannot save a film that has a rotten performance, but performances that are truthful and delivered with conviction can save a film in which the technical quality is mediocre.

Not only is the actor indispensable—he is irreplaceable. If the camera breaks down, the filmmaker rents a new one, and if the cameraman gets sick, he finds somebody else, but if the actor walks off his set after he has established him in a role, he has nothing. The actor knows this, and when his back is against the wall it is his only defense and he will use it.

The actor works with his body and his voice. When he is in difficulty he suffers and the filmmaker must be equipped to help him. If the filmmaker cannot help, there will ensue the temperament and tantrums that have destroyed so many films. Working well with actors is a special gift which the filmmaker must cultivate. The way he solves the problems of his actors is of much greater consequence than anything technical he may do.

Some people think of actors as neurotics, sick people who make a career out of pretense. Others think of them as beautiful children who must be manipulated. The truth is that acting is a noble profession, and that actors satisfy a basic need of mankind. Ever since man came out of the cave, there have been people who have stood up before other people and pretended to be someone else. The phenomenon of theatre is found in every culture, and feature motion pictures are, among other things, another medium in which the mysterious collective need for "performance" is fulfilled.

AFI

In this age of munificence it is only natural that the filmmaker look to the foundations for money. Unfortunately there isn't very much around. There are two or three Guggenheim Fellowships available to filmmakers each year, but the competition is enormous and the selection process inscrutable. The Ford Foundation flirted with filmmakers a few years ago, but has now taken to supporting The American Film Institute. AFI, as it is called, is really the only place where "free" money is to be found.

Started in the middle of 1967 with an initial capitalization of more than $5,000,000, the AFI has expanded rapidly. One must applaud its various archival and custodial projects (locating lost masterpieces, preserving old films, and cataloguing the entire output of the American cinema), its "internship program" (see "Visiting the Set"), assistance to educational institutions, and various programming efforts around the country. As for the two functions of most interest to the filmmaker—the production grants and the Center for Advanced Film Studies—it is still too early to submit a final verdict, but the AFI must, at this moment, get mixed reviews.*

Both efforts are of great importance, and are certainly well intentioned. The problem seems to be a

* The author confesses to having been the recipient of two grants from the AFI: one for screenwriting and the other for production. These grants were extremely helpful and the author expresses his gratitude herewith. Despite this, the comments that follow are meant to be objective.

certain Kennedyesque tendency toward overpromise, a predilection for elegance and public relations at the expense of real accomplishment. The AFI guards its image with jealous care, and its offices, stationery, and surprisingly large staff are most impressive. However, it can be said of the AFI that there is less there than meets the eye.

For those who have received them, the production grants have been enormously helpful. But many talented people with worthy projects have been turned down by the AFI, and it is unfortunate that some of these people have received savage treatment at the hands of AFI staff members.

Some impressive announcements were made a few years ago about how the AFI was going to finance a number of low-budget films with major-company money, to the extent of $400,000 per picture, with the distribution guaranteed. Unfortunately nothing has been heard of this lately, and we are told that no worthy projects were submitted. This is the same nonsense we've been getting for years from the studios, which set up "talent development" offices and then disbanded them because, they told us, they couldn't find good scripts.

To present the problem as concisely as possible, one has the impression that if an American Godard walked into the AFI today with a concept as innovative, brilliant, and contemporary as was *Breathless* in 1959, he would be laughed out of the office. This has probably already happened, and what a tragedy that is.

The Center for Advanced Film Studies is a quite marvelous concept. Unfortunately, instead of being housed in some crummy warehouse that might provide an appropriate ambience, it fills a lavish mansion in Beverly Hills. It's amusing to walk around this place, where marble halls resound to the steps of eager and ambitious young filmmakers, cursing the establishment and speaking bittersweetly of their plight. They have fine facilities, superb screening rooms, access to any film they wish to see, entree to the most prominent filmmakers in America, and sympathetic instructors. What they don't have, and what they really want and need, and what is the most urgent problem for the young filmmaker in America, is money for production. At the AFI that, it seems, is in short supply.

By all means apply to the AFI, for funds and for a Fellowship, but be forewarned that you will be given a terrifying scrutiny, and your chances of getting help are limited.

Agents

In theory, an agent is someone who admires your talent, gives you love, warmth, and protection, and develops your career. In practice, you will find that the amount of admiration and love you receive is directly proportional to your income. This should come as no surprise since agents work on a commission of 10 percent, and their own careers depend upon the amount of billings they achieve. Thus their attention is lavished upon clients who make six-figure incomes, and you, the junior filmmaker, are at the bottom of the heap.

One might well ask: is it not in the interest of agents to discover and develop young talent so that they may reap profits in the future? It is, and that's the only reason they'll talk to you. But remember:

the agent uses a buckshot approach—he signs as many young people as he can, and hopes that one of them will turn out to be profitable.

A lot of young filmmakers will say, with some pride, "I'm represented by William Morris," or CMA, or IFA. The question is not "Which agency represents you?" but "What has your agency done for you?" and the answer usually, is "Nothing." Shortly after signing a contract for exclusive representation, and waiting around for those big offers you thought were implicit in the deal, you call your agent and find you can't get him on the phone. There then ensues several months of being similarly "savaged" and the consequent feelings of impotence, frustration, and rage.

A filmmaker needs an agent. The following notes may assist him in finding a good one:

(1) **Young agents.** The problem with young agents is: (a) they are scared, because the large agencies are terrorist organizations with intricate office politics and occasional mass firings; (b) they are also hungry, and therefore interested only in increasing their billings so as to increase their own salaries; and (c) what kind of a young man goes into something like this anyway?

(2) **Look for a heavy.** (See "Juniors and Heavies.") A heavy has seen it all, is impressed by nothing, makes lots of bread, and has no reason to lie. If he thinks your script is lousy, he'll tell you. If he says he's going to move on something, he'll move. There are very few young heavies.

(3) **A real heavy.** One of the heaviest agents in the business, when asked what he does for a living, always

replies, "My game is ten percent." He has no pretensions about being a developer of careers or a friend of artists. He sees himself as a salesman, which is precisely what he is; he is proud of it, as he should be; his clients make a lot of money and so does he.

(4) **You have to hustle your hustler.** You're going to have to sell and pressure and hustle just as much with an agent as without one; you're going to have to continue to excite your agent, because the moment he gets bored, there's nothing in it for either of you. The question arises: if I have to hustle my agent, why don't I drop the middleman and spend the same energy hustling principals? Answer: he has access you don't have because it's his business to be friends with people you wouldn't care to spend much time with, and, despite what you may think about your business acumen, you should never negotiate for yourself.

(5) **Contracts.** If you are dealing with one of the large agencies such as William Morris, CMA, or IFA, which insist on having their clients under contract (some of the best agents at smaller agencies work on verbal understandings), then keep in mind the following: (a) don't sign until the agency has actually done something for you, or at least lined up something firm, and (b) don't sign a contract for more than one year's representation. The agency won't like either of these stipulations, but if they don't give in on them, they're not that interested in you and you can be sure of being savaged later on.

At the same time they ask you to sign an exclusive agreement the size and weight of a telephone book, they'll tell you that there's nothing to worry about because these weighty contracts can always be broken by mutual consent of the parties. If you think these statements contradict one another, you're right. It's neither easy nor pleasant to get out of a contract for representation, and that's why a contract that comes up for annual review makes a great deal of sense.

(6) **Don't expect your agent to offer you anything.** Your agent won't offer you anything because you're not in demand. What he *can* do is get your projects around, and get your work exposed. When you've spent months setting up a deal that he closes in ten minutes, you may well ask yourself why he should get 10 percent. The answer is that for all their faults, agents get you more money than you can ever get for yourself, and thus earn their commissions many times over.

(7) **On being angry with your agent.** One hears people say, "I'm so pissed off at X, I'm never going in there again!" Well, that's where he's got you: he couldn't care less.

(8) **Figure it out for yourself.** If your agent is anything above a junior, he's making at least $25,000 a year. He has a secretary who gets at least $6000. He takes up space in a rented office, makes frequent use of the phone with lots of long distance calls, ties up messengers and Xerox machines and screening rooms. It's got to cost a minimum of $40,000 a year, and probably a lot more, just to keep him in the office. To break even, then, he has to book a minimum of $400,000, and breaking even isn't most people's idea of doing business. So, figure it out: just what are you worth to him with a screenplay that might be sold

for $10,000? Not very much. The client structure of an agency is a pyramid and naturally he hopes you'll be worth $100,000 in a few years. Right now he represents you on speculation, and the minute you begin to look like a loser is the minute he begins to lose interest.

(9) **Exceptions.** Of course there are exceptions. There are agents who are humane, who care deeply about their clients, and who may, in some strange way, live vicariously through them. The thing to look for in an agent is this kind of caring, and real enthusiasm—a sincere interest in you and your talent. If you can find an agent who will give you that, then you will have found a treasure beyond value.

Audiences

For the filmmaker there is no sensation quite so exquisite as to sit anonymously with a paying audience in a theatre and feel that audience respond to his film. Audiences are strange. They seem to emit an energy of their own, and when that energy is in tune with the energy being emitted from the screen, one can sense a oneness between audience and film, a "resonance" that is thrilling. When people laugh when you want them to laugh, feel anxious when you want them to be anxious, and move with your story at the pace at which you unravel it, there is a feeling of intoxication that makes all the pain of filmmaking worthwhile.

Much has been written about the fact that the majority of the film audience is now under twenty-five years old. This audience is referred to by studio executives as "the kids," and these same executives would give everything they have if they could discover the secret of what makes these "kids" want to see a picture.

Actually there is no great amorphous horde that can properly be called "the kids." Of the millions of young people who lined up to see *Easy Rider* and *The Graduate*, only a fraction were inveterate film-goers, the hard core whose word-of-mouth can create a hit. There are many varieties of youth audiences, many classes and sub-classes, including those who will go to see *Woodstock* and those who will sit through the most tendentious works of Godard, those who will never attend a subtitled foreign picture and those who want to see nothing else.

The problem that production and distribution executives have in understanding the audience is a problem they have brought upon themselves. They are too lazy to go to the theatres and find out what's going on. They prefer, instead, to look at pictures in screening rooms. Young filmmakers like to do this, too, when they get the chance, perhaps because it gives them a feeling of being "in," and also because of the ridiculous notion that they should be able to see movies without paying.

The only way to understand the audience is to go to theatres, to stand in line on Friday and Saturday nights with everyone else, to sniff around and see what's happening. These expeditions can be fascinating. After a while, if you go to everything, you begin to sense the kinds of audiences attracted to different kinds of pictures. You become sensitive to the look and the feel of different types of people, and you begin to understand what works for an audience and what does not.

If the distributors did this, and if they were sensitive

observers of the human scene, there would be many fewer disasters at the box office. The filmmaker is urged to mingle with audiences for a different reason. He should be interested in them not because of an obsession with the particular conditions of the marketplace, but because audiences are his lifeblood. Whether he wants to please them or unload upon them, insult them or flatter them, if he is to achieve "resonance" he must understand who they are and how they are affected by film.

Bankability

Bankability, being "bankable"—acceptable to the bank, which usually means acceptable as a low risk to the studio management—is one of the most important things that can happen to the filmmaker. Once he has achieved bankability, he can do what he wants. No more hustling, no more hype, no more scrounging around and being degraded by the businessman. When he is bankable, he simply proposes his project, and the funds become available to carry it out.

Unfortunately there are very few filmmakers who are completely bankable. The list varies from year to year, and rarely numbers more than half a dozen. At the moment we might say that Mike Nichols, Arthur Penn, John Schlesinger, David Lean, and Stanley Kubrick are bankable. Next year the names may be different. There was a time when Otto Preminger, Billy Wilder, Elia Kazan, and William Wyler were on the list; today one cannot be certain that they are. Some of the finest directors are only bankable to a limited extent. Ingmar Bergman, Orson Welles, and Federico Fellini are considered risky for different reasons: Bergman because his films seem to attract a small if devoted audience; Welles because he is considered grandiose and irresponsible; and Fellini because, although he has hit it big several times, his methods make businessmen feel insecure. Sidney Lumet is probably bankable only to a limited extent; Jean-Luc Godard, the most important film artist of the decade, is probably not bankable at all. Alfred Hitchcock is still bankable, but not so much as he was before.

It is all very mysterious. Somewhere, in somebody's safe, there must exist a black notebook that tells exactly how much money can be safely risked on a particular director. This notebook is undoubtedly looseleaf, because as each picture comes out, the relative degrees of bankability are altered.

To become bankable one must hit and hit big. If a director makes a picture that earns upwards of $15,000,000 he is getting near to complete bankability. It helps if he has hit more than once. If his last picture earned $7,500,000, he may be bankable, but there is still a limit to what he can spend. It is even more complicated, however, because there are subtle psychological factors at work. To hit big may not always be enough. There are hits that can be rightly characterized as flukes; there are successful directors who are considered unstable and who do not inspire confidence; and there are others with long and steady track records who just don't come off as "heavies."

It used to be true that stars were the bankable

people. Some still are, but things change fast. It's no longer enough to have Burt Lancaster in a film, or Gregory Peck, or Shirley MacLaine, or Rock Hudson. Jane Fonda is highly bankable but Henry Fonda is not. Paul Newman, Steve McQueen, and Barbra Streisand are a lot more bankable than Doris Day and Sean Connery, whose names, a few years ago, were magic on the marquee. For a long time people thought that Elizabeth Taylor was bankable. Now, after a run of money-losing pictures, it doesn't make much sense to pay her $1,000,000 and a percentage of the gross. Dustin Hoffman hit it big, twice, in *The Graduate* and in *Midnight Cowboy*. He's very bankable, but in five years he may have worn thin.

What does it all mean? Not very much, really, except that the attainment of bankability is an ephemeral thing that has nothing whatever to do with talent. If you are thinking about working on a large scale, in the area of several million dollars, you are either going to have to attain a significant degree of bankability, or be packaged with someone else who has.

Breaking Through

If you want to be a doctor, you go to medical school, serve as an intern and a resident, and begin to build a practice. If you want to be a lawyer, you go to law school, meet with recruiters who come to the campus, join a firm, and work your way up to a partnership. If you want to write or paint or compose, you sit down, create some work, and if it's good, people become interested in you and you begin to build a career. But if you want to be a filmmaker, it's a different story.

There are no recruiters coming to the film schools, and the expansion of the economy has not been accompanied by a need for more film directors. You can't just sit down and make a film, because you need a lot of money for even a modest effort. The profession of filmmaking is small and exclusive, and there is no direct or traditional route to it. The filmmaker hustles and struggles as best he can, and if he is lucky, he finally makes a breakthrough. Here's a brief rundown on some of the different ways it has been done:

(1) Crossing over from within the film industry. Many directors have crossed over from other areas of filmmaking:

SCREENWRITERS. Of all the various fields from which to cross over, screenwriting seems the most obvious. The writer is, after all, a creative artist, and a storyteller. The move from author to film auteur could not be more natural. Among the many who have taken this route are: John Huston, Joe Mankiewicz, Billy Wilder, Abe Polonsky, Richard Brooks, and, among the younger directors, Francis Ford Coppola.

SCREEN ACTORS. Although acting is a performing art, and therefore less close to directing than screenwriting, the actor has many opportunities to observe the filmmaking process. Many actors, dissatisfied in the role of soldier, have tried to play general. For some, like Marlon Brando and John Wayne, it has been a one- or two-shot effort. For others, it has been a significant breakthrough: Paul Newman, Gene Kelly, Jerry Lewis, Charlie Chaplin (the great master), and among important younger directors, Mike Nichols, John Cassavetes, and Dennis Hopper.

CAMERAMEN. Quite a few cameramen have tried to direct films. They know how to set up the shots, and they certainly know how to photograph things in a handsome way, but directing requires an intellectual power that few of them possess. Of those who have succeeded, George Stevens is the most significant in the older generation, and Haskell Wexler in the younger.

FILM EDITORS. A few film editors have made the crossover. Most of them were only in editing for a short time: David Lean, Robert Wise (who edited *Citizen Kane*), and among the younger ones, Karel Reisz and Anthony Harvey.

FILM PRODUCERS. Many producers yearn to direct, but when the chips are down, most of them don't have the nerve. One who did was Stanley Kramer. Of the young producers-turned-directors, Alan Pakula may be the most significant.

(2) **Lateral entry from a related profession.** A traditional way of becoming a film director has been to move over from a related field. Years ago they came from the theatre; today they come mostly from television:

STAGE DIRECTORS. Joshua Logan, Peter Brook, Otto Preminger, Elia Kazan, Arthur Penn, and many others.

TELEVISION DIRECTORS. This would seem the most obvious means of lateral entry, and many directors have broken through this way. Strangely, the process has slowed down in the last few years, possibly because television in its earlier days was an exciting medium that attracted and nurtured talent, while today it is a factory operation and most TV dramas look as if they were made by the same man. Among the many directors who have come out of TV are: John Frankenheimer, Stuart Rosenberg, Robert Mulligan, Sidney Lumet, Richard Lester, Norman Jewison, Elliot Silverstein, Sydney Pollack, and Robert Altman.

(3) **Apprenticeship.** In Europe many filmmakers started out as assistants and apprentices to established directors. The most famous example, of course, is Federico Fellini, who worked as an assistant to Rossellini. For some reason this system doesn't work in America. In the entire history of Hollywood only a couple of assistant directors have made the breakthrough.

(4) **Some oddball routes.** William Wyler was once a publicist. Peter Bogdanovich was a film critic, as was François Truffaut and many other French New Wave directors. Andy Warhol is a painter; Norman Mailer is a novelist; Roman Polanski attended the Polish film school, made a feature that became an international success, and quickly moved to the West; Shirley Clarke, Lindsay Anderson, Alain Resnais, and Gillo Pontecorvo made documentaries.

(5) **Making an independent feature.** Finally, there is the low-budget independent feature, a uniquely American method of breaking through. Of the many who have gone out and made a picture with whatever money they were able to scrape together, only a few have returned with a success. But this method has launched a number of important and promising young directors, some of whom had to attempt the venture more than once: Stanley Kubrick failed with *Fear and Desire* and *Killer's Kiss*, but finally made it with *The Killing*; Brian De Palma failed with *The Wedding Party* and *Murder à la Mode*, but finally made it with *Greetings!*; Frank Perry did it with *David and Lisa*;

Robert Downey with *Putney Swope*; Paul Williams with *Out of It*; and John Korty with *Crazyquilt, Funnyman,* and *Riverrun.*

Cameramen

The cameraman, along with the actor, is the most important artistic collaborator of the director, and along with the production manager, he is the most important member of the production crew. A cameraman can make or break a film, particularly certain types of low-budget films that are dependent upon their visual quality. The speed at which he works has a great effect on the cost of a film; his reliability affects the psychology of the filmmaker; and his manner and disposition affect the morale of the entire production. He is an important man, and on a low-budget film where he is both director of photography and camera operator, his importance is crucial.

Some notes on cameramen:

(1) **There are many bad cameramen.** Since the work of a cameraman is not ephemeral, but is measurable by objective standards, it is remarkable how many bad ones are walking around making a handsome living. A cameraman may be bad for many reasons: he may be difficult to work with, bitter because he is not a director, constantly provoking power plays in which he attempts to take over a production; he may be a sloppy craftsman who gives inadequate care to his

equipment, tries to "eye-ball" the exposure, constantly jams magazines, and runs out of film in the middle of a shot; he may be a prima donna; he may lack physical energy and begin to die after lunch; he may be more interested in making love with the leading lady than in doing good work; and he may simply be untalented, unable to frame, unable to light, and willing to settle for second-best. The list of faults is endless but the point is that there are many bad cameramen around, and the stories of what has happened to people who have used these fellows are bloodcurdling.

(2) **What to look for in a cameraman.** Aside from talent, which is obvious, there are a number of qualities to look for in a cameraman:

EXPERIENCE. A cameraman should have shot many hundreds of thousands of feet of film. On anything but a student production it is insane to go with a newcomer.

VERSATILITY. In screening the work of a cameraman, look for an ability to work in different styles. What you need is a man who can translate your conception into visual terms; not one who imposes a single rigid style on everything he shoots.

RESPONSIBILITY. The cameraman should take full responsibility for the care of his equipment. A cameraman who does not notice an uneven pressure plate, a scratched lens, or a rundown battery is worthless.

MECHANICAL ABILITY. On a low-budget film, a cameraman who can take apart and repair a camera on location is worth his wage many times over.

PHYSICAL STAMINA. The cameraman works hard, and often under grueling conditions. A good cameraman is extremely strong.

LOVE OF CRAFT. A good cameraman loves his

work; he likes nothing more than to shoot film and look through the view-finder. Unfortunately, there are cameramen who don't love their work at all.

ABILITY TO COLLABORATE. A good cameraman should make plenty of suggestions, but suggestions that are relevant to your intention. A cameraman who spews forth ideas that have nothing to do with what you want is not a true collaborator.

ABILITY TO INSPIRE CONFIDENCE. A good cameraman has the confidence of the actors. They know he knows what he's doing, and that he is not going to make them look bad.

LEADERSHIP. The cameraman runs the crew a good part of the time. Like the director, he must have qualities of leadership.

ABILITY TO IMPROVISE. Great cameramen improvise and invent, constantly. When faced with a difficult problem, they do not throw up their hands but set to work to find a solution—to find enough light, somewhere, to make the shot.

(3) **The cameraman and photographic style.** There are many different ways to shoot and many different ways to light. In selecting a cameraman, the filmmaker must know what he wants in the way of photographic style.

Older cameramen of the Hollywood school like to work on sound stages. These are the gentlemen who can give you that gloss we associate with Hollywood—"Rembrandt Lighting," that look where every blade of grass is lit all the way down the road. They need many assistants and cutters and flags and lights. Although one must respect them for their craft, one must realize that they are totally irrelevant to the low-budget feature.

Among younger cameramen, there are inventors and innovators, highly adaptable to location situations, able to render a scene in numerous ways. A perfect example of this type is the brilliant French cinematographer, now turned director, Raoul Coutard, who shot most of the films of Godard, several of the best films of Truffaut, and *Z*. Coutard is a filmmaker's dream, a man who can work with a small amount of equipment, does most of the setting up himself, is quick, versatile, and constantly produces work of the finest quality. The thing about films photographed by Coutard is that they all look exactly "right"—that is to say, his photographic style is always in tune with the content of the film. Thus, unlike the rigid stylists of the Hollywood school, the new cameramen are active collaborators of the filmmaker. Rather than presenting him with a particular "look" with which he must work, they develop a "look" that becomes part of the filmmaker's concept.

If you want a "documentary look," by all means consider a good cinéma vérité cameraman who is used to working with a hand-held camera. If you want a "mysterioso" look, as, for example, in a horror film, or a dramatic look for a police story, or a "big sky" look, as in a Western, you should definitely talk to people who specialize in these styles. But keep in mind that on a low-budget film a cameraman who is obsessed with matching shadows is not going to work out. He may be able to give you the style you want, but at a cost in time that you cannot afford. This is one of the problems of style: it costs money.

(4) **Pretty pictures.** In the last ten years films have become very handsome. Today we rarely see a film that does not look good. This kind of quality, which

used to be exceptional, has now become the norm, and as a result it has become less striking and less important.

Handsomeness in film is now available to anyone who has the money. Pretty pictures can be bought. It's merely a question of long shooting schedules, skilled people, and lots of equipment. But what, in the end, does it mean? Ken Russell's *The Music Lovers* is extraordinarily handsome. There are scenes in this picture, particularly certain scenes in a forest, that are of unbelievable beauty. But the film is basically rotten, and all its prettiness cannot redeem it.

On a low-budget film you cannot afford to buy pretty pictures. The money is simply not there. What you have going for you is the originality of your story and the excellence of your performances, and these are qualities that are less a product of money than of talent. In planning a low-budget film there is a great deal to be said for going for straight lighting—lighting that illuminates the action in a pleasing way, and that looks natural. This involves a sacrifice, because one would always prefer to wait for the sun to be in a certain place. However, "low budget" means compromise, and because prettiness cannot support a picture, this may be one sacrifice worth making. Good, clean, clear definition may be the inevitable photographic style of the successful low-budget feature.

(5) **The relationship between the cameraman and the director should be one of collaboration.** A cameraman who says "yes sir!" all the time is not very helpful, and one who is constantly argumentative may be even worse. An ideal collaboration is difficult to achieve, but even when there is some conflict, things can work out if the relationship is based on mutual

respect. The cameraman knows that the director is the boss, but on the set they work hand-in-hand to achieve the director's concept. A director who has to bully his cameraman, or who does not have total faith in him, is in as much trouble as the director who leaves a leadership vacuum for the cameraman to fill.

There will be times when you, as the director, will want to operate the camera. On these occasions the cameraman will graciously defer, and he will be overly helpful in getting everything ready so that you can operate with a minimum of technical fuss. But at the moment you inform him of your desire to operate, he will say to himself, "OK, let's see what he can do that I can't handle." This is the normal reaction of a man who is proud of what he does. So be it; if the relationship is good, the cameraman will give you a slightly ironic smile and there will be no further repercussions.

Casting

(1) Casting is one of the most important functions of the filmmaker, and it depends totally on his ability to judge the potential of other people.

(2) On a low-budget film casting is a particularly exhausting process because there is no money to pay a casting director to go out and bring back selected actors with proven talents. On a low-budget production one usually works from an "open call," and the resulting procession of out-of-work actors with their glossies and résumés and attention-getting devices is really beyond description. It is all worth it, however, when

someone turns up whom the filmmaker recognizes instantaneously as the person he wants to play the part.

(3) One usually asks actors who look interesting to "read." One may give them portions of the script to take home and prepare; one may improvise with them; watch them improvise with each other; test their emotional risibility; observe their responses; and note how well they take direction. One should do all of these things, testing and probing in as many areas as one can, but in the end the most important quality to look for in an actor may be rapport: are you going to be able to work with this actor on a basis of intimate friendship? When a film is shooting and the pressure is on, friendship and understanding may be the qualities that have most to do with failure or success. When the filmmaker goes with someone of limited experience whom he genuinely likes, he may be taking a smaller risk than if he had chosen an experienced professional with whom he did not feel much rapport. Then, too, the filmmaker should remember that one of the important things about shooting a picture is that it be fun, and that this is possible only when one is working with one's friends.

(4) It was widely believed for many years that a person looked different on film that he did in real life, and the only way to discover whether he came off on the screen was to conduct a screen test. This may have been true when most films were black and white, and when filmmakers were looking for star quality and glamor. On a low-budget production a filmmaker may be more interested in ensemble playing and other qualities that can be determined without a screen test, but screen testing, which is very inexpensive in 16mm., has certain advantages. For one thing, it preserves a

reading for further study and can be of great help in making a final decision between two or three apparently equal people. It also gives the filmmaker a chance to appraise an actor very coolly—something that is difficult to do when the actor is playing to him instead of to his camera.

(5) Some young male directors have a tendency when casting female roles to be seduced by superficial beauty and overt sexiness. Fashion models, who are notoriously bad and mannered actresses, often turn up at casting calls, and the filmmaker who falls into the trap of going for the clotheshorse when the part requires talent, or being carried away by big breasts when the part requires an expressive face, is a fool who cannot distinguish between what he needs on the screen and what he thinks he needs in his bed.

(6) When a part requires nudity it is wise to explain this from the start. It is a mistake to think that an actor is going to play a nude scene well if he has to be coaxed and/or tricked into doing it.

(7) The two big theatrical towns, New York and Los Angeles, are filled with undiscovered actors and actresses of genuine talent who will work for very little in return for a chance to be in a feature film. They will also give the kind of devotion and commitment to a production (perhaps because they are young and hungry) that is rarely obtained from a major star. These two qualities, devotion and commitment, cannot be bought at any price, and their value to a filmmaker who is working with a small budget is inestimable.

Cinéma Vérité

Of all the breakthroughs in film in the 1960s, cinéma vérité may be the most important. Out of it has come a new genre of films that has changed our understanding of the word "documentary." At the same time, cinéma vérité has raised complex psychological and moral questions about everything from the way the presence of a camera alters the reality before it, to the extent to which the filmmaker is entitled to be a voyeur.

One of the most interesting side effects of cinéma vérité is the way it has affected the big screen. In feature films, now, it has become general practice that when you want to portray reality—as, for example, in a combat sequence—you must shoot your scene so that it simulates documentary newsreel coverage. Otherwise, if the camera is too steady, if it does not shake when there is an explosion, if anything has the slightest look of having been "lit," people will see that it is false and they will not suspend their disbelief.

Ironically, the coverage on television of the war in Vietnam has not changed most filmmakers' ideas about how combat scenes should be staged, but only about how they should be shot. We therefore find ourselves in the strange position of looking at films in which the acting and staging and situations are transparently phony, but the camera coverage is realistic. Cinéma vérité, then, has affected us less in our perception of the truth than in our conception of how the truth should be depicted. As a result, there exists in the subconscious of the audience an absurd equation that says film graininess plus an unstable camera equals reality.

Clichés

The thing about film clichés is that before they became clichés they were brilliant innovations. Because they were brilliant they caught the fancy of other film-makers, and degenerated into predictable motifs.

We are amused by old films when we see things like: the quiet and mysterious stranger riding into the Western town whom *we* know is the fastest gun alive; the great burglary film that ends ironically with all the money blowing away in an enormous wind; montages of newspaper headlines and railway wheels showing the passage of time; and the key line from the historical melodrama that usually goes something like, "Boiled milk, Louis? All of Paris is laughing!"

But are these any less comic and predictable than:

the hero or heroine, alienated and existential, taking a long walk through the streets of a modern city, observing the riffraff of humanity clinging to the edges of deserted piazzas at midnight;

the lyrical sequence, with rock music over, in which the lovers ride a bicycle, walk along a beach, or cavort in an idyllic meadow;

the homosexual friend to whom the girl confesses her heterosexual difficulties;

the unexpected encounter with the peasant whose lined face exudes earthy wisdom;

the quarrel at the family dinner table that exposes the generation gap;

the sequence in which angry and stern-faced blacks tell off the establishment;

the film that ends when the young hero hits the road with knapsack and thumb to discover the brave new world of the counter-culture?

Although these story clichés have all become sickeningly familiar, their remedy is simply more imaginative writing and conceptualization. But clichés of style present a more difficult problem. Over the last decade we have seen some brilliant innovations on the screen, stylistic ideas that, when first used, excited us enormously. Already many of them are becoming clichés:

violence depicted as a ballet in slow motion (brilliant in *The Wild Bunch* and *Bonnie and Clyde*, now standard and tedious);

subliminal frames representing states of mind (exciting in *Hiroshima Mon Amour*, tendentious in *The Pawnbroker*);

flash-forwards (remarkable in *Petulia*, reaching their final corruption in such television series as *The Mod Squad*);

shifts of focus as different characters speak (incredible in the tent sequence in *Lawrence of Arabia*, nauseating in *Getting Straight*);

using titles in the middle of a film (creative shorthand in the films of Godard, excuses to spring a commercial in *The Man from U.N.C.L.E.*);

extensive use of the telephoto lens (powerful in *The Battle of Algiers*, merely pretty in *The Thomas Crown Affair*);

breaking down the barrier between screen and audience by having a character suddenly address the camera (startling in *Alfie*, loathsome in television commercials);

ending a film with a freeze-frame (moving in *The 400 Blows*, now as standard as superimposed main titles).

The problem here is not that these stylistic ideas can be used only once, but that they must be used with purpose. Filmmakers who deal in flash grasp onto them and misuse them, degrade them and turn them into clichés, and thereby steal them from other filmmakers who are hesitant to use them even when they are appropriate.

Closeup, The

There are filmmakers who will tell you, "When in trouble, go for a closeup." Their films are series of closeups, one after the other, huge magnified images of the human face responding over and over again in the same way. In addition to punishing the audience by inducing a sensation of claustrophobia, their reliance on full-face closeups to tell a story may be the certain evidence that they are hacks.

Television is the medium of the closeup; on the small screen it is always effective. But on the big screen of the movie theatre the closeup must be used with restraint or else it loses its power and becomes meaningless. Closeups are important, and when used properly among the most powerful of images, but when the filmmaker uses them too often he may find himself in the middle of a climactic scene with no place to go.

In addition to this problem of exhausting effectiveness through overuse, there is also the problem of the actor. Actors who are inexperienced in film often don't realize that playing to a closeup is a special art. Stage actors, particularly, will tend to over-project. The filmmaker must not let this happen. The normal expressiveness of the human face can become ludicrous when it is blown up hundreds of times onto a huge screen. In film a flash of an eyelash can be more expressive of human agony than any kind of "projected" contortion. This leads, however, around in a circle, because if the actor must understate, then he is, in that process, limiting the number of things he can do with his face. The result is that even the best closeup acting can become monotonous, which is another reason why the closeup should be used with restraint.

What, exactly, does a closeup mean? When we see a cut to a closeup, we are being told, in effect, "This moment or this reaction is very important and I want to make sure you see it." There are times when this becomes terribly obvious, and in such cases a camera move into a closeup can be much more subtle and effective than a straight cut.

Many directors do not consider themselves covered on a scene until they've shot closeups and closeup reactions on all their characters. They feel safer with these closeups in hand, and they may be right. In the cutting room closeups are indispensable material if an editor has to do major surgery on a scene, but it seems both silly and wasteful to shoot a lot of throwaway closeups without any intention of using them except as protection.

Collaboration

Nobody can write, produce, direct, shoot, edit, and star in his own picture. Orson Welles came close with *Citizen Kane*, but he needed the help of his brilliant cameraman, Gregg Toland, his co-author, Herman Mankiewicz, and his editors, Robert Wise and Mark Robson. The point is that filmmaking is a collaborative art. The filmmaker is essentially a director who may have some skill in writing or acting, but there will be talents he does not have, and to provide these he will need collaborators.

How he chooses the people he works with and how well he relates to them is the essence of his collaborative talent. Collaboration is a skill that does not come naturally to many artists. If a filmmaker cannot collaborate, if experience reveals that he cannot work well with other people toward a mutual goal, then his career may become jeopardized very fast.

Color and Black and White

There was a time when the filmmaker had a choice between shooting in color or in black and white. Unfortunately that time may now be past because black and white, for all its beauty and the essential stylization of its images, is a dying format on the big screen. Black-and-white features are just not considered commercially viable anymore, particularly in respect to that most important subsidiary right: sale to television. A filmmaker should, by all means, try to shoot his picture in black and white if that's what he wants to do, but he should be forewarned that what may look like a way to save a great deal of money may make the raising of money much more difficult. The word, unfortunately, is out, and investors know that black and white, commercially speaking, is death.

Commercials

One of the more glib statements that one hears is the oft-repeated, "The best thing on television is the commercials."

It is only by a supreme stretch of the imagination that the TV commercial has been elevated to an art form. This has been accomplished through the uniquely American process by which an industry creates awards and festivals with which to pat itself on the back. If there is a festival for TV commercials with golden statuettes and parchment certificates, then, of course, the commercial *must* be art.

Many false and even invidious comparisons have been made between commercials and other things, such as "brilliant gems," "cameos," and even "poems." This is to suggest that because a commercial runs sixty seconds and costs $60,000, its overstudious craftsmanship puts it in the same league as "Ode on a Grecian Urn."

Directors of commercials are fond of pointing out that if a TV set is left on in a nursery school, the children will pay most attention to the commercials. It must say something about their need for acclamation that they have set up pre-school children as arbiters of quality. Doubtless, to a three-year-old the plastic Icarus of Eastern Airlines is more interesting than *Bridge on the River Kwai* or the funerals of our assassinated leaders, but this is not convincing proof that commercials are the best thing on television.

Commercials are about deodorants and mouthwash, cigarettes and automobiles: devices that either conceal our animal nature or else kill us off before our time. No matter how brilliant the parody in, say, an Alka Seltzer commercial, in the end it all comes down to an upset stomach. High-camp style imposed upon content that is insane and degrading to the human spirit, motivated by the greed of a huge corporation, intended to swindle the public into buying something it neither wants nor needs—that is what commercials are all about.

On directing commercials: A number of filmmakers have taken this route, hoping to move over to features at an appropriate moment. A feature by Barry Brown, a hot-shot director of commercials, entitled *The Way We Live Now* might give them second thoughts. Whereas in a commercial all is flash and style, and characters are created by casting archetypes who suggest a life-style through a single moment of caricature, the full-length film must have structure and story and character development. The difference between sixty seconds and one hundred minutes is so enormous as to make experience in the first length irrelevant to success in the second. There is also an old-fashioned belief which may have a great deal of merit: the sellout to advertising is so corrupting that no return is possible; it quickly burns up the human reserves needed to create works of art.

For these reasons commercials may be the worst place for the filmmaker who wants to make features to start out. He can suffer enormous damage by working in this mannered form, and if he falls into the trap of believing that commercials are important, he will be all the more likely to fall on his face if (and it's a big "if") he does get a crack at a feature.

Competition

The would-be filmmaker should have no illusions: competition in the film industry is stiff and it is tough. In the United States less than three hundred feature films are released each year. Most of these are made by experienced directors. Despite what you may have read recently about the doors opening up, the fact is that the young and inexperienced director is still suspect and he is still expected to prove himself. No one is handing out hundreds of thousands of dollars and total artistic control to young men who want to make films. In an average year there is room for two or three new directors—in an extraordinary year, four or five. All you have to do is think of all your friends who want to make films, and then of all the kids everywhere who want the same thing, and you can figure the odds for yourself. Look around any room of film students and tell yourself that not one person in the class is likely to have a chance to make a feature; if you do that, you'll have a realistic view of just how tough the competition is going to be.

Craftsmanship

One of the most depressing things about a lot of student films is their lack of craftsmanship. This does not mean that every film has to be "well made" and everything has to match and every cut has to be smooth, but it does mean that there is no excuse for really bad technical work, bad exposure, bad framing, bad focus, bad sound, indecipherable dialogue, sloppy editing, thumbprints on the negative, gouges and scratches, etc., because these things are usually not the result of lack of money but of lack of craft and lack of pride.

There may be a mystique attached to this in certain circles—filmmakers who deliberately deride craftsmanship and utilize crudity of technique to carry a stylistic message. This is all right, and for a short period of time it may even provide an interesting reaction to Hollywood, but, in the end, bad craftsmanship reflects a contempt for film, and it is inexcusable.

Critics

Among film critics there are fools, acid-throwers, gun-slingers, neurotics, and cultists, as well as men and women of intelligence, perception, and taste. Most of the major and "high-brow" critics have assembled their reviews into thick and expensive volumes, and when we read them (by Macdonald, Adler, Crist, Kael, Simon, Sarris, and the rest) there is a strange disappointment, for, really, there is very little to be learned from these writings and it is doubtful that there is a filmmaker alive whose perception of his medium has been affected by them.

Of course, we are not their audience; they write for the general public. But even so, we must often find them guilty of shallowness. To give just a couple of examples, how can one explain the lavish praise they gave to the mediocre *Z*, and the much more restrained praise they gave to the infinitely better *The Battle of Algiers*? Or, how come *The Wild Bunch* appeared on the ten-worst lists of several very prominent critics, when it was clearly one of the best pictures in its particular year?

Fortunately the important critical pulpits—*The New York Times*, *Time*, *Life*, *Newsweek*, and *The New Yorker*—are held by decent and intelligent people. Still, despite the good taste and excellent prose style of many critics, when we come right down to it, they are parasites upon us. They make their living commenting upon our work, and although they serve a necessary function, and in the case of the small, independent, and not widely publicized feature, they can be extremely helpful, still, they exist because we exist, they eat off of us, and knowing this we cannot help but feel a certain superiority.

This feeling is reinforced when we read things written by the best critics which we, as filmmakers, know are not true. They often have no technical knowledge and may praise a cameraman for things done by a director; or blame a director for things done by an obstreperous star; or criticize the quality of a film when it was the quality of the projection that was at fault. They tell us that a certain director has submitted a disgraceful performance, without any conception of the incredible pressures under which he may have worked. They write of a director as if he had total control over a film when often he has not, and they blame him for things that may have been inserted by some idiot in studio management.

There is only one sane way to deal with film critics and that is to ignore them. Sure, appreciate their praise, and be grateful when it helps a picture and makes it possible to make another, but remember: if you believe them when they rave about you, you must also believe them when they pan you. And since they are human, and therefore prejudiced and fallible like anyone else, it is best to think of them as a necessary evil—people who are, like the executives of major companies, the natural enemies of the filmmaker.

Dead Ends

The beginning filmmaker should be wary of taking jobs in the film industry that are not directly related to what he wants to do. When he starts off, he may be willing to take any job he can get, just for a chance to work with film. This is probably wise, but he must avoid becoming trapped in a comfortable position that offers financial security but which is, ultimately, a dead end.

Some examples of dead ends:

FILM PUBLICITY. People go into this thinking it will

help them make "contacts" that will prove useful later on when they announce they are filmmakers. Their "contacts," who will have become accustomed to thinking of them as publicists, will not be useful; they will laugh.

TV COMMERCIALS. (See "Commercials" for a full discussion.) This field is an end in itself, and it doesn't lead to personal relationships in the feature-film industry.

MAKING INDUSTRIAL AND EDUCATIONAL FILMS. There are many jobs available in the field of sponsored films, and many people take them when they start off. It's not a bad place to begin: one can make a handsome living and at the same time gain experience and learn technique. There are hundreds of small film companies that engage in this kind of work, and there is hardly one where the boss isn't talking about that little feature he's going to make. On the surface his ambition makes sense, since the company usually owns equipment and is viable as a producing organization. The fallacy: making a feature is like shooting dice and small entrepreneurs are temperamentally unsuited to taking the necessary risks.

THE STORY DEPARTMENT OF A MAJOR COMPANY. Lots of promising young people take jobs as story editors and script readers, hoping to get close to the action. This makes sense if you want to be a producer, but if you want to be a filmmaker, major companies, or other kinds of office situations, are not good places in which to be.

TALENT AGENCIES. The same as major companies —OK for prospective producers; death for the filmmaker.

TELEVISION NEWS AND DOCUMENTARY DEPARTMENTS. Better for the cameraman than for the director.

MISCELLANEOUS ODD JOBS IN EDITING AND COM-
PLETION FIRMS. One finds a lot of prospective filmmakers working in sound studios, running the dubbers
or the projector; in music and effects editing; in equipment rental firms; and even in film laboratories. Of all
the dead ends, these may be the most depressing.
These jobs lead only to bitterness and frustration.

TEACHING FILM. This can be a stimulating career
in itself, but unless you're doing it as a part-time
means of survival, it is very much a dead end.

To sum up, there is a job market in film, and there
are decent salaried jobs available, but in the end, if
you want to put something on the big screen, it's better
to earn $75 a week running coffee for Arthur Penn, or
working as a grip on a low-budget independent feature,
than to make $300 a week editing somebody else's
documentary on muscular dystrophy. The filmmaker
should beware of jobs that are comfortable and secure.
His chosen profession is neither, and although the
seduction of a pleasant and well-paid job can be great
in those many inevitable moments of despair, he must
resist the temptation to settle for half, over and over
again. It is the essence of the strength of will that he
needs not to allow himself to become dead-ended.

Deals

Everything in film revolves around the "deal." If you
go into film, you can expect the pattern of your professional life to follow a scenario: you will initiate
projects and projects will be offered to you; there will
be many, many calls between you, your agent, pro-

spective producers, and studio executives; all of these calls will revolve around the question of whether somebody else is ready to make a deal.

A deal, however, once it has been made (assuming, of course, that no one has blown it), can mean even less than the ridiculous conversations that led to its consummation. Studio managements constantly welsh on their commitments, and even a contract confirming a deal can be worth less than the paper it is written on. The favorite way of ending a deal is for someone to look into your eyes and in a controlled, subdued, level voice say, "If you're really unhappy, then sue us."

This dare should be taken at face value. Often it will cost a management less to face a law suit than to keep a bargain. Law suits take years to be resolved, and in the meantime money is de-committed from your project and used to make profits which, if you do have a case, can be used to pay you off later at less than the original agreed-upon amount.

The deal is everything, therefore, and also nothing. You can't start shooting until you've made a deal, but even when you have a deal you may not be able to shoot.

Deferments and Percentages

One hears a great deal of talk about deferred salaries and percentages of profits in lieu of money "up front." These are devices used by producers and studios to cut their costs and to entice people into working for less than they would normally receive. A frequent statement is, "If you really care about the project, you'll defer half your fee; otherwise we just won't be able to make it." The trouble is that ninety percent of the time deferments don't get paid, there are no percentages because there are no profits, and the person making the statement is not deferring anything himself.

Another bad thing about deferments and percentages is that getting them depends upon the honesty of people who are notoriously dishonest. You're not going to see any money unless you get an honest count. (See "Honest Count, An.")

If you are offered a job on the basis of a deferment or a percentage, it should be settled in your own mind that you're not going to see another dollar. Then, if the job still seems interesting, you can take it, having become psychologically prepared for the likely result.

It is wise for the filmmaker acting as his own producer not to con the people with whom he is going to work. If he is honest with them and tells them straight out that if any money is made they will share in it but that the odds are not good, they will appreciate his good will and their incentive to work will not be affected.

If one has a choice between offering a deferment or a percentage, the percentage is preferable. The problem with deferments is that it's always understood by the person who defers that he will be paid out of the first moneys received. When there are other people in the same position (actors, laboratories, other crew members) it becomes a question of who will be paid in what order. The resulting hassles are very unpleasant and the legal work can cost thousands.

Finally, on a low-budget independent feature film, it's absurd to pretend that people aren't working for less than they deserve. If their major interest is money, then they are not right for a low-budget production. In return for their commitment and devotion, the filmmaker owes them, at the very least, an honesty that is unknown in the filmmaking-industrial complex.

Designing Shots and Coverage

A lot of directors talk ominously about the struggle to get "coverage"—about the pressures of time that make it difficult to shoot sufficient "coverage" to tell a story with film. This approach to directing—that it somehow revolves around "coverage"—leads to a great deal of hack work. It is also symptomatic of directors who are insecure, who are afraid to use their shooting time to execute a personal idea, because they fear that later, in the cutting room, that idea might not work out.

It is the director's job to tell his story with film, and when the director is good, his shots are designed to tell the story in a way that has a particular meaning. The director who shoots a standard series of set-ups on every scene (master, medium shot, closeups, and reverses) is one whose work looks pedestrian and who is better suited to a job on a television series.

To cover a conversation between two people with a series of over-the-shoulder closeups is to take an easy route and to risk blandness. Experience has proven that such shots will, indeed, cut together smoothly, and that the scene will, for all practical purposes, play. But that is hardly enough. The director is supposed to use his camera to express himself, and when his scenes are brilliantly staged but covered in an ordinary fashion, he is doing only half the job.

Every scene must be thought out from the point of view of exactly what shots best express its meaning, and how certain shots may express the filmmaker's view of his material. This second approach will result in the film's having a sub-text, conveyed by its style. There are directors who can take second-rate material provided by a studio and turn it into something interesting by expressing various degrees of irony, contempt, or whatever, merely by the way they shoot.

A perfect example of a designed shot is the scene in *Five Easy Pieces* where Jack Nicholson sits down to play the piano. Bob Rafelson, the director, pans down to his hands, then across the piano, very slowly, to the reaction of Susan Anspach, and then even more slowly across a wall filled with framed memorabilia, including snapshots of Nicholson as a boy, then back to Susan Anspach, and finally back to Nicholson. The result is that in a single shot the director has movingly expressed a complicated series of ideas about a man, his past, and his attitude toward his past, without a single word of dialogue and in a manner that can only be described as a *tour de force*.

The reason Alfred Hitchcock is so widely admired by French *cinéastes* is because his shooting is designed —his shots are original and expressive and executed with an artfulness that is not flashy but which conceals itself. Although Hitchcock shoots from storyboards (which may indicate a lack of spontaneity on the set), his films warrant the full attention of the filmmaker interested in understanding the meaning of designed shots.

Directing

The director must, of course, have talent and brilliant ideas, but if he cannot apply his talent and execute his ideas, he is a director only in name. The act of directing, as opposed to "being a director," is almost irrelevant to talent and to art. Directing is the process by which the filmmaker realizes his ideas by getting other people to carry them out. Directing, then, is the achieving of a concept, and this is a function of leadership.

Directors provide leadership in a great variety of styles, and their methods are generally consistent with their personalities.

There are directors, for example, who are extremely domineering, who are strict disciplinarians, and who run their sets and extract performances by their forcefulness and by the degree to which they inspire fear. Some people respond to this method very well: either they yield to superior force, or else they use their detestation of the director as inspiration for doing good work. The film director with the heavy German accent and the riding crop in his hand is a cliché, possibly patterned after Erich von Stroheim, who not only was a tyrannical director, but also impersonated in *Sunset Boulevard*. Among contemporary directors, Otto Preminger is reputed to be of this type.

There are other directors who work with gentleness and kindness, who make love to their actors in a figurative sense, and who create an aura of loving on their sets. They are soft-spoken and seductive. People work well with them because they are inspired by love and affirmation. Jean Renoir may be the prototype, and François Truffaut is said to be a practitioner of this style.

There are directors, like Elia Kazan, who use a psychoanalytic approach, who get deeply involved with actors, for whom they become confessors and confidants. The actor feels that he has a special relationship with his director, and the director, in turn, is able to use this intimacy to wrench out of the actor's subconscious a deep, startling, and truthful performance.

There are other directors who work with their competence, their cool, and their charm. They are delightful gentlemen and they are leaders by virtue of their attractiveness. Such men are Fred Zinnemann, George Cukor, and David Lean.

There are directors who lead by virtue of personal mystique. Men like Federico Fellini and Orson Welles inspire awe. Their reputations as great artists and the flamboyance of their personalities ignite and energize the people around them.

There are directors who are loose, who turn their sets into playgrounds, who may even use practical jokes to relax people and reduce pressure. This kind of disarmament of anxiety has worked very well for Mike Nichols.

There are directors who are great instinctive group-dynamicians, who turn their sets into communes in which everyone has a say and the approach to a scene is worked out through discussion and agreement. The actors who were in *M*A*S*H* say that Robert Altman used this method. He may be the prototype for young directors who wish to explore that most intriguing development of youth culture"—the "leaderless" communal style.

There are directors who inspire by their enthusiasm and their bounce, their boyishness and their energy; there are others who indulge in somewhat corny attempts at being "one of the boys," playing poker with the grips, going to football games with the gaffers; there are those who are remote and mysterious, who create an aura of deep thought and implacability; there are directors who are sly and tricky and directors who are snarling and vicious. In the end it does not matter what technique a director uses, as long as he gets what he wants. Whether he provides leadership by coercion or seduction, mystique or charm, the result on the screen is what is important. To achieve that result he should use whatever style is best for him.

It is impossible and even distasteful for a young filmmaker to sit down, consciously analyze his own character, and from that analysis deduce a correct style of directing. Directors usually arrive at their techniques by unconscious and undeliberate means, and may change their manner from picture to picture, as they discover through trial and error their weaknesses and strengths. Directors who fail at achieving their concepts are usually the ones whose images seem false to the actors and crew and whose hypocrisy loses them respect. When people working on a picture sense that the director is a private masquerading as a general, the result may be in doubt, because leadership is intrinsic to directing, and where there is no leadership, there is no director.

Director as a Culture Hero, The

The film director has become a modern culture hero. He seems to have replaced the novelist and the painter and the great virtuoso musical performer as an international celebrity. Only the rock music star provokes more intense emotions and has a more zealous following. The film director is treated by the high-brow media as the *ne plus ultra* of contemporary artists, a man who works with ideas, people, and images, who creates works of art that have a profound impact upon culture and upon people's lives. Film is the medium of now, and, as they say, "it's a director's medium."

There may now be reason to believe that the heroic and superstar qualities of the film director have become over-rated. For years the concentration was on movie stars: it was a Liz Taylor picture, or a Clark Gable picture, or a Humphrey Bogart flick. Now it is a Fellini, an Antonioni, a Nichols, or a Kubrick. Of course, it is correct to think of the filmmaker as the author or *auteur* of a film. The question is not whether the filmmaker is the central artist in the creation of a picture, but whether his influence upon the cultural scene is as great as some people like to think, and whether his image as a superstar is appropriate to the development of the cinema. It may be time for the prospective filmmaker to examine these questions, for they relate to some of the wrong reasons that people have for going into film.

In the first place, it is difficult to find one film a year that could become an important artifact of our civilization in the way that many paintings are representative artifacts of nineteenth-century France, or novels of nineteenth-century Russia, or music of nineteenth-century Germany. When one looks at a list of the ten greatest films of all time, as these lists are occasionally drawn up by critics and film buffs, one finds that certain titles constantly recur: *Potemkin*, *Citizen Kane*, *The Bicycle Thief*, *La Grande Illusion*, etc. All these films are important works of art, but one wonders about their cultural significance in relation to contemporary works in other media: the works of Picasso, for example, or of Stravinsky, or of James Joyce and Thomas Mann. The fact is that film is a young medium which for all practical purposes did not exist until this century, and that many fewer films are made than books written or paintings painted. Still, no Shakespeare has, as yet, made an appearance in cinema, and there has never been a film that has shaken and moved and galvanized America as much as John Steinbeck's *The Grapes of Wrath*—including the film of that same title. This is not to say that film has any less potential than other forms; just that its potential has not yet been fully realized.

People frequently say they were "moved" by a particular film. It is encouraging to hear this, but one wonders exactly what they mean. Many good films seem to stay with people for a few days, and then begin, rapidly, to fade away. When seen again on late-night television, pictures that once seemed important are often disappointing, their impact diluted by time and changing fashion. Aristotle's classic evocation of the theatre as a place where man is purged of anxiety by undergoing pity and terror in the presence of tragedy, would seem applicable to film with its huge domineering screen, its ability to direct the eye and to powerfully stir the emotions. But for some reason such a deep experience rarely takes place in the movie theatre, even in the presence of masterpieces of cinema.

Why, in all the fine American films of the past few years—and America has taken back the leadership in creative filmmaking—in such pictures as *Bonnie and Clyde, Easy Rider, Midnight Cowboy, M*A*S*H, They Shoot Horses Don't They?*, and many other superior works, why, out of all these pictures, are there so few great and memorable moments? Why is it that the impact of our best films has been limited to the summation of a prevailing mood as opposed to the ability of works in other media (i.e. the record album *Highway 61 Revisited*) to, literally, change people's lives? Why, for all the talk about film as art, are motion pictures still generally looked upon by the public as a means of escapist entertainment, as some sort of luxurious form of TV, as "pop?"

One cannot be sure of the reasons. Perhaps, to expect a masterpiece every year when only two or three hundred films are released is to expect too much. Perhaps we have overrated the potential of the cinema. Perhaps film is a superficial form. The most likely reason, however, is that there is something wrong with our filmmakers, and it is here that the phenomenon of the film director as a culture hero has a certain relevance: there are too many young people who want to be film directors because it is the glamorous thing to be, because, as in the twenties it was the thing to go to Paris and write a novel, now it's the thing to go to California and make a film. When we read about the huge sums earned by important directors, the glamor and celebrity that accrue with success, the director's image as a combination man-of-action and artist, we can be seduced by fantasies of the filmmaker's life-style and crave to be like Fellini with all of Europe at his feet.

The fact is that masters of the cinema like John Ford and Alfred Hitchcock did not think of themselves as cultural superstars. They thought of themselves as picture-makers, and their greatness as artists was in no way affected by their lack of star consciousness. Perhaps now it is time for the filmmaker to shed the useless paraphernalia of celebrity and concentrate once again upon the work at hand: raising the level of the cinema, making film an immediate and consciousness-changing experience. The potential is there but not enough good films are being made. The filmmaker must stop believing what the media have told him about himself: that he is important and that he has a profound effect upon the culture of the land. His job is to make great pictures, and too often, while he bathes in the adulation of his press, those pictures go unmade.

Sure, if you hit it big, you want it all—the adulation, the adoration, the money, the fame—but it is well to consider how quickly directors burn themselves out, how the best films of many directors are cluttered into a few short years before the mannerisms and the affectations and the self-parodying begin. The stresses of the profession are fantastic. The filmmaker should look at what this combination of professional pressure and stardom has done to many rock musicians, how it has destroyed them as people and as artists. Perhaps it is time to stop the nonsense of the film director as a culture hero; perhaps it is time for the filmmaker to seek a more secluded, and austere life-style dedicated more to the creation of great pictures and less to the enhancement of himself as a star.

Distributors

Of all the bad people in the film industry, distributors —the men who market a film, and place it in theatres —are among the most wicked and dishonest. Distributors, unfortunately, are necessary. Until filmmakers get themselves together and devise a system of film distribution under their own control, they will suffer as they always have at distributors' hands. But since distributors are at present a necessary evil, the filmmaker must know and understand them in all their heinous complexity.

Some notes on distributors:

(1) **It is easy to get distributors to see your film.** It takes only a couple of hours of their time, and they cannot afford to refuse to look at anything that is offered to them. To get them to a screening you do not need an agent or a contact or anything else. You simply call them up and set up a time. However, if you describe your picture in terms that do not sound commercial, they may send over a junior salesman. The trick in inviting a distributor is to tell him that your film is like *Love Story* even if it's more like *The Seventh Seal*. It doesn't make any difference. Just say it's like the latest hit that comes to mind, and you can be sure that a herd of reptiles will descend upon you.

(2) **Remember: it's a buyer's market.** Unless your film looks highly saleable and blatantly commercial, and has attracted the interest of several companies,

the distributor is in the strong position. He knows that without him you cannot hope to recoup anything, unless you try to distribute yourself, in which case you must risk a minimum of $30,000. He also knows that after making an independent feature you are most likely broke and in debt. Assuming he's interested in what you have, he will offer you the least attractive deal he can devise, which usually includes no cash whatsoever in advance, no guarantee of any kind, and other terms so tough as not to be believed. Usually you are not in a position to negotiate an improvement, which is not to say you shouldn't try, but only that you should know that he knows he's got you over a barrel.

One might well ask what kind of a system it is, in which a filmmaker must go out and risk everything to make a picture, and then when it's all finished and looks good up there on the screen, be at the mercy of businessmen who squeeze him for all they can get. The answer is that it's a rotten system, and it will have to be changed soon.

(3) **Distributors have no interest in film as art, or in giving the public an opportunity to see good films.** Their sole interest is profits, and therefore their judgment of a film is based solely on how they evaluate its commercial appeal. They will frequently tell you, "That's a beautiful picture, kid. Too bad it's not going to make money. Next time try to work in a little more tit." They will pat you on the back and suggest you call them again when you've made something else.

(4) **Since distributors are not interested in quality, the problem comes down to convincing them that your film is commercial.** This is extremely difficult to do, because distributors, for all their talk, are

extraordinarily stupid about the realities of the market-place. Nearly all of them turned down *Z*, which had been proven a success in Europe, because they thought it would be a loser at the box office. When Cinema V finally picked it up and made it into a smash hit, one would think they might have learned a lesson, but they didn't and they probably never will.

The trouble with distributors is that they are totally irrational in the way they judge the commercial value of a film. They are so out of touch with the people who actually pay to see movies that they lack the expertise necessary to make correct business decisions. They look at the figures in *Variety* as they might look at the *Daily Racing Form,* and they try to play the market on the basis of tips, hunches, and their own personal taste—all of which constantly misleads them. There is one distributor who relies solely on the advice of his wife; there is another, quite substantial, who has been known to buy pictures after he's slept through them.

The only way to overcome this kind of irrationality is to try to show a film in an audience context, with ringers in a screening room, or, taking a chance, as a sneak preview in a theatre with a paying audience. Sometimes, but not always, good preview cards and a favorable audience reaction will convey to distributors an impression of commercial viability.

You must also remember that your film may well *not* be commercial, and that its appeal may be very limited. This doesn't mean that it can't do business, but that it must be carefully distributed, or, as they say in the business, given "special handling." Nothing scares distributors more than the idea of "special handling" because they are neither professionally nor intellectually equipped to treat a film in any but the most obvious way.

(5) **Distributors often blow a picture because they open it and advertise it incorrectly.** The ignorance of distributors about the basics of their own work is truly incredible. There are times when they completely misunderstand the market for a picture and try to play it off in situations where it hasn't got a chance. Thus we find a film like *Hi Mom!* opening and failing in two huge Loew's theatres in New York, with heavy and wasteful advertising, when it should have been booked into a small Greenwich Village art house and publicized extensively in the underground press.

(6) **Any contract with a distributor should be examined by an attorney who specializes in film work.** Most negotiations end in an agreement that is more or less favorable to the distributor and detrimental to the independent producer. But even so, the precise and exact wording of the contract should be closely scrutinized by a lawyer, because in addition to taking advantage of you with a bad deal, distributors will play dirty tricks on you later on if your film is a success. They will do this by evoking obscure clauses and interpreting the contractual texts in ways that are advantageous to them and disadvantageous to you.

(7) **Be certain your distributor guarantees you a proper opening.** Because it is a buyer's market, it is only in those rare cases when a picture looks hot that a distributor pays a producer an advance "up front" against earnings, sufficient to recoup all production costs. In the usual case, when there is no cash advance, the distributor should be made to guarantee that he will spend a sufficient amount on advertising and promotion to assure a film a reasonable chance of success. The minimum figure for an opening in New York is

$30,000, and $50,000 is a lot better. The distributor, in advancing this kind of money, becomes involved in the general risk-taking that is essential if a film is to attract attention; the greater his investment, the less likely he may be to "dump" you after a first bad week at the box office.

(8) Distributors will steal you blind; the object is to keep the stealing down to a reasonable 10 or 20 percent. To illustrate the kinds of things that can happen, let's suppose that a small, independently produced feature costs $100,000, and does $1,000,000 worth of business at the box office (which is not at all bad for a small film). Of this $1,000,000 box-office gross (see "Exhibitors" for a discussion of the various ways the theatre owners steal from the distributors; i.e., although $1,000,000 may be reported by the theatre owners, the film may actually have done a third again as much), approximately 30 to 40 percent, or $350,000 is returned to the distributor in the form of "film rentals." "Film rentals," then, are the moneys taken in at the box office minus the exhibitor's expenses and his share of the take. Now this $350,000 is received by the distributor and immediately applied against "distribution costs." It is here that most of the stealing by the distributor takes place.

"Distribution costs" are defined as those expenses incurred by the distributor in releasing a film. They include advertising, promotion, prints, etc., and in our example they could mount up to $200,000 of the $350,000 received as rentals. Now these charges are supposed to be accountable, and when one receives a statement to the effect that $200,000 has been spent on "distribution costs" one's first instinct is to demand an audit. The results will be amazing: you will find badly kept records, or missing records attributable to a convenient "fire" in the office; there will be false receipts and charges that cannot be explained. In some cases there will be records and books in such extraordinary condition that it may cost tens of thousands of dollars to get to the bottom of them. Huge "distribution costs" may be the result of kickbacks and other under-the-table deals, all disguised by vouchers and receipts it could take a private investigator years to disprove. In short, the area of "distribution costs" is where you get robbed, and the process of uncovering the theft is expensive, time-consuming, and usually comes down in the end to a straight dare by the distributor to sue him.

We are left, then, with $150,000. To this the distributor applies his 30 percent distribution fee, which is supposed to cover his overhead and operating costs. This uses up $45,000 and leaves $105,000 of "profits." These profits are then split in accordance with the distribution agreement (in which the relative percentages may change as the profits exceed certain plateaus). In a normal case the first $100,000 may be split 60/40 in favor of the producer, so that in our example the producer receives back $63,000 or less than two-thirds the cost of his film, on a picture that was made very cheaply and has earned ten times its negative cost at the box office.

How can something like this happen? Nobody knows, but it has been happening for years, and it is happening to somebody right now.

Distributors will savage you in other ways. They may commit to paying a guaranteed amount over a certain period of time; then, if your picture fails (which may be due to their mishandling of it), they will welsh on the deal and dare you to sue them. And if your film is an enormous success, they may withhold your money for months and even years on the pretext that collections from the exhibitors are "slow." In the meantime they will be using your money to finance some sex-epic of their own, which will fail miserably, drive them into bankruptcy, and make them permanently "uncollectible."

To sum up: If you happen to see your distributor sitting in a plush restaurant, cutting into a large steak and guzzling drinks in the company of a beautiful, expensive woman, you may be tempted to believe that every cent he's spending is being charged to "distribution costs" on your picture—and you may very well be right.

(9) **A new kind of distributor.** In reaction to the stupidity, dishonesty, and generally disgusting performance of most distributors, there has sprung up in the last few years a few new, young distribution companies predicated on giving the filmmaker an honest count and keeping expenses to a reasonable level, and run by the kind of people who make pictures and go to pictures. These companies usually work on a straight 50/50 split after expenses, which instead of running 60 percent of rentals, may consume less than 20 percent. Most of them specialize in the nontheatrical market, but they are a marvelous breath of fresh air in a foul wilderness, and there is hope that soon they will take over the business and revolutionize it.

The only other solution is for filmmakers to get together, organize a distribution company, staff it with people who are their employees instead of their partners, and distribute their own pictures. Unfortunately filmmakers aren't temperamentally suited to the distribution business, but some kind of viable cooperative may be the only answer to their needs.

(10) As of this time, there is no way for a film that is not commercial to be distributed in the United States. It is possible to get some money back on worthy noncommercial films of limited appeal through the so-called college circuit, but as of now the film-maker who makes pictures of quality that do not have popular appeal is in a bad way. Not only is financial recoupment a major problem, but just getting his films on a screen before an audience is extremely difficult. Some people are willing to put up with this for a while, but there comes a time when one gets tired of making good pictures and not being able to show them. There must be a solution to this problem, and if there is one area where the American Film Institute has a function, it is to devise a way for worthy non-commercial films to be distributed in the United States.

Documentaries

In the past ten years cinéma vérité has so changed our conception of the documentary film that the classic documentaries of Robert Flaherty, Pare Lorentz, and John Grierson are more interesting as artifacts than for what they can teach us about the documentary form. There coexists with cinéma vérité (or truth cinema, or direct cinema) another form of documentary which most younger filmmakers rightfully find repugnant: the beautifully photographed 35mm. color documentary with its serious and self-consciously artful voice-over narrator and its evocation of false poetics through the use of sunsets and sunrises and staged sequences. Fortunately this type of film is confined to that sub-species of documentary known as the "industrial" and to the film departments of government agencies. Cinéma vérité is where it's at, as far as documentaries are concerned, and great cinéma vérité films must be recognized for what they are, which is masterpieces of film editing.

Gimme Shelter may be one of the best cinéma vérité documentaries ever made. Produced by the Maysles brothers, brilliantly edited by Charlotte Zwerin, it has a powerful, almost devastating effect when shown on the big screen. Part of the reason for this may be that unlike many cinéma vérité features, *Gimme Shelter* is structured like a fiction film and affects its audience like a Greek tragedy.* The stars are The Rolling Stones, and these daemonic young men, with irresistible charisma and magical power over their audiences, are followed on their journey toward the inevitable tragic denouement at Altamont. The ending of *Gimme Shelter* has much in common with the ending of *The Bridge on the River Kwai*—the coming together, for perfectly rational reasons, of diverse elements (Rolling Stones, Hell's Angels, and hippies) in a finale of madness and doom.

Gimme Shelter proves that the documentary feature can be more exciting than the fiction feature film. For this reason, and also to gain experience in shooting and other technical processes, the young filmmaker interested in theatrical features should not rule out the possibility of documentaries. Of all the ways to begin a career, working in documentaries may make

---

* The Maysles' other documentary feature, *Salesman*, had similar characteristics. Zwerin cut it as a story and the salesmen are presented in the opening titles as actors portraying themselves. There is something too obvious, however, about discovering the psychic void at the center of a bible salesman's life, and *Salesman* ends up being heavy and pretentious.

the most sense. The filmmaker should realize, however, that great documentarians are great because they do nothing else. They are not interested in making fiction features, and their devotion to and mastery of their form should not be taken lightly or thought to be easily attainable.

In the end the great difference between the cinéma vérité documentary feature and the fiction feature (including the "documentary" fiction feature, e.g., *The Battle of Algiers*) may be defined as a matter of control. The documentarian exerts control at only two points: when he picks his material, and in the editing room where he uncovers the story he has shot. For this reason, editing, in the documentary, may constitute at least 60 percent of the creative input. The fiction filmmaker has control throughout: on the screenplay, on casting, in his ability to plan and stage and reshoot his scenes an unlimited number of times. For him the most creative phases are in writing and shooting. This difference in the extent of control should not be underestimated. It comes down to a matter of temperament: the man who enjoys creating a fantasy, who wants to make his own world and people it with his own characters, versus the man who interprets life by looking into the real world, finding a story of real people, and then shaping that reality into a personal vision.

Dropping Dead

When a film opens, gets terrible reviews, and nobody comes, we say that it has "dropped dead." Filmmakers to whom this happens prefer to say "my film went down in flames." To "go down in flames" is a false evocation of the romantic, employing imagery that connotes martyrdom. When you say "my film went down in flames" you can hold up your head and laugh. It is a convenient psychological device, and if it spares you notions of suicide, then by all means use it. The truth is that your film "dropped dead," and there is nothing worse.

Editing

(1) Everyone knows that editing is an important part of the filmmaking process, and that there are certain films reputed to have been "made" in the cutting room that are constantly held up as proof of the editor's power. The use of the clock motif in *High Noon*, the creation of the loudspeaker as a major character in *M*A*S*H*, and the musical selections over the transitional traveling sequences in *Easy Rider* are three common examples.

There have also been instances when a straight story was reconceived by a film editor: when subliminal flash-forwards were cut in to give thrust to a film with a slow beginning (*Petulia*), or when a film was restructured by taking the ending and using it as the opening in order to reframe the story as a flashback (*Lolita*). Filmmakers have drastically altered performances and relationships between characters by editing and cutting, and in the very process of selecting takes they have made basic decisions that have established or altered the mood of a picture.

What is less known, and of particular relevance to the filmmaker working on a low-budget feature, is the ability through editing to make a scene play quite differently than the way it played at the time of shooting. Naturally, once a conception has been imposed upon a scene by a director, it is difficult to shake it off, but on a small feature where inexperience and monetary pressure will inevitably lead to the failure of some directorial intentions, this ability to cut a scene for a different result is very important.

(2) Something that is obvious but needs constant restatement is that before you cut a scene you must know what you are cutting for. When a scene does not work as it was intended, it is necessary to scrutinize the raw footage very carefully from a variety of new angles, to discover if there is something of merit that can be used. For this reason it is wise for a filmmaker not to dominate his editor, but to work in collaboration with him. A fresh pair of eyes will often see something to which the director is blinded.

One of the most amazing and mysterious things that happens in film is that there are scenes that turn out better when recut from a new point of view than if they had worked out as they were written, rehearsed, and shot. In the cutting room the filmmaker must not be rigid; he must be flexible enough to exploit this phenomenon because it may provide him with a last chance to save his film.

(3) One normally makes a cut when (a) one wants to show the audience something not contained in the shot that is on the screen, or (b) when one wishes to establish a different point of view, or (c) when a

shot is losing its energy and it is necessary to re-energize the screen. This third contingency can be called the "tyranny of the cut"; it occurs when an editor is forced to employ the artificial convention of an instantaneous change in point of view when there is no logical reason for such a change. The convention of the cut becomes particularly tyrannical when a scene between two or more people must be broken up in order to sustain the interest of the audience. This often leads to the destruction of fine acting moments and usually is necessary because the director has merely "covered" his material, instead of designing shots that expressed it well.

Experienced filmmakers instinctively work for energy within the frame so that screen energy does not have to be provided by cutting (except, of course, in action sequences). Some young directors overcome the "tyranny of the cut" by employing various and sometimes contrapuntal levels of action in the foreground and background planes. Their pictures are made up, in large part, of long, sustained takes which do not bore the audience because they are brilliantly performed and ingeniously designed. Then, when it is time for an action sequence, the sudden use of many rapidly cut images has, by contrast, all the more force.

By working in this way they obviate the artificial distinction between "master shots" and "cut-a-ways," and, in effect, they cut their films in the camera. On a low-budget picture this method can save a great deal of money; the shooting ratio is lower than when a director uses a more academic approach. It also reduces editing to a more subordinate phase, comparable to what it was in the days before the filmmaking theories of Sergei Eisenstein became dominant.

Ego Trips

There are several films around these days that have no value except as ego trips for their makers. An ego trip on film occurs when someone comes to believe that his fantasies about himself are of interest to other people, and that the very fact that he has fantasies is sufficient justification to put them onto film.

The difference between the fantasies of Federico Fellini in *8½* and *Juliet of the Spirits,* and those of Norman Mailer in *Wild 90, Beyond the Law,* and *Maidstone,* is the difference between films that are important and exhilarating and films that are boring and silly. Fellini is a master of the cinema—his entire life has been devoted to film—and when he shares his fantasy with us in *8½,* it is by means of his craft, his creativity, and his commitment as a film artist. Mailer, on the other hand, is an important and brilliant writer who has decided to dabble in film, believing that excellence in one medium may be transferable to another; he presents his fantasies to us without craft or art or commitment to anything but the enhancement of his own ego.* Mailer is certainly entitled to do whatever he wants with his money, but there is too much unfunded film talent walking around for any real filmmaker to respond to what he does with anything but contempt.

---

* It is interesting that when another writer, Truman Capote, turned to film, he did not indulge himself with an ego trip but made a modest and well-intentioned documentary on capital punishment.

Another kind of ego trip has been occurring recently, which may be even more insulting to filmmakers and degrading to the screen than Mailer's films. A young person, heir to great wealth, sets out to fulfill the fantasy of so many of his contemporaries (i.e., become a film director). He does not begin by learning the craft, or studying film, or paying his dues like everybody else; he begins by financing a feature film which he directs and in which he stars as himself in a fantasy about his own life.

This kind of activity is masturbatory and worthless. It is based not only on the assumption that his fantasy is of interest, but also on the even more insidious assumption that anyone, talented or untalented, artist or nonartist, can and should make a film. Mailer, at least, has proven himself as a superior man of letters; he has created fiction, and in the literary medium has turned his fantasies into art. These rich-kid-film-director types (best left unnamed) don't think it's necessary to prove anything about their talent, even to themselves. Convinced that their pedestrian daydreams are the stuff of art, they treat film with neither reverence nor commitment, but rather as a game or a fad.

There is nothing wrong with financing one's own pictures if one can afford to do so, but it becomes a serious question of taste when a totally inexperienced and frivolous person, without any trace of talent or knowledge of film, with nothing except money, degrades the struggle of serious filmmakers.

Equipment

(1) Young filmmakers are fascinated by equipment and dream of owning some of the marvelous devices with which one makes a film. This hang-up on equipment can lead to a "studio complex." Paramount and M-G-M have only recently awakened and disposed of their equipment inventories. What the filmmaker has that is valuable is his talent and his energy and the story he wants to tell. He should remember that one good story is worth more than $100,000 worth of cameras and lights.

(2) Equipment should be rented when it is needed; when one is not using it, it is worthless and ties up capital better applied to the production of films. An obsession with equipment can also become an excuse not to think about important things, such as what one is going to do with it.

(3) A lot of people are seduced by expensive and elaborate editing machines like Kellers and Steenbecks. Unless one is opening an editing and completion service, they are an unnecessary luxury and are merely convenient. *Potemkin* was probably cut on a viewer; *Citizen Kane* on an old-fashioned Moviola. The Keller or the Steenbeck editing table will not make a film work; only a good editor can do that, and all he needs is a second-hand Moviola and splicing tape.

(4) The only exception to the general proposition that one should not buy equipment applies to the

cameraman, who should, if he can afford it, own his own camera.

(5) Even on the lowest budget productions, equipment is not a good place to try to save money. One should never rent more than one needs, but one should never go to an equipment rental dealer just because his prices are low. There is nothing worse than a lousy camera with an uneven pressure plate or an inexact light meter or magazines that scratch and rip film or a lens that is soft or a tape recorder that does not produce sync. No matter how brilliant a cameraman may be, he is worthless with bad equipment.

(6) One of the more amusing moments in low-budget filmmaking occurs when one picks up equipment at the freight entrance of a rental house under the hostile eyes of a gang of theatrical teamsters. These situations often erupt into classic confrontations between long-hairs and hard-hats, and symbolize better than anything else the essential change that is taking place in the filmmaking profession.

Etiquette

Film etiquette is something that does not really have to be explained. Sensitive people grasp it intuitively. Unfortunately, however, there are people who act improperly on a film set, perhaps because they are insensitive, perhaps because they regard good manners as middle-class and boring and counter-revolutionary. For their benefit, here is a short list of propositions that have mostly to do with the attitude of production crew members toward their director:

The film director is the boss of the set. If he wants an opinion, he will ask for it. If he wants to turn his set into a commune, he will do so. But until he indicates a desire for either of these things, comments should be limited to helpful suggestions.

What you do and say off the set is your business; what you say on the set, even if it's nonverbal, should be consistent with the mood set by the director. There's a famous scene in *Citizen Kane* when Welles begins on Susan Alexander, performing at the Chicago Opera, then moves his camera up vertically to the catwalks of the theatre where two stagehands hold their noses, expressing their derision of Miss Alexander's singing. Unfortunately one sees this kind of thing on the sets of major studio productions, where experienced union stagehands, who should know better, roll their eyes and make other nonverbal comments behind the backs of performers and directors. Sam Peckinpah has said that it is a privilege to work on a motion picture and he is right. Such behavior is intolerable, and anyone who indulges in it should be thrown off a picture.

Never bring a stranger or a guest to the set without the director's permission. The set belongs to the director, and no one is welcome there without his consent.

When you say "no" to a director, be sure you have a good reason. Directors often demand the impossible, and it is the duty of everyone working on a film to try to provide it. Before you say it can't be done, you should have tried very hard.

A technician should not give artistic advice to an actor. If, for example, an actor is speaking in a very low voice, and the sound man would prefer that he speak louder, he should relay this thought through the director. For him to instruct the actor to speak up is a usurpation of directorial authority.

Crew members and authorized visitors to a set should be very careful about catching an actor's eye, or snapping a still photograph in the midst of a take. These things can destroy an actor's concentration. It obviously follows that when nude scenes are being performed and other highly sensitive acting situations arise, the crew should behave extremely well.

At an invited screening it is very bad form to groan, hiss, or express derision in any way. When you pay for a ticket, you can do anything you want; when you accept an invitation, you should behave as a guest in the director's house. If, after the screening, your host asks for your opinion, then, of course, you can say what you want.

All of these things are obvious, and one could go on forever with a list of dos and don'ts. The general thesis is that the set and the film belong to the director; when he invites you to collaborate with him as an actor or technician, to visit his set, or to look at his picture, he is paying you an enormous compliment and extending to you his most precious gift, which is his work. In return, he has a right to expect your courtesy.

Exhibitors

Fortunately, the filmmaker rarely has to deal with the people who own and operate movie theatres: the exhibitors. They are the problem of distribution companies. But if you think distributors are bad, wait until you meet a few exhibitors. Here are some of the things they do:

(1) **Exhibitors steal money from the people who supply them with films.** One of their classic methods is to keep a double set of books. Theoretically, every ticket sold is taxed, and therefore to falsely report one's gross receipts is not only a breach of contract with the distributor, but also a crime against the government. The possible consequences do not seem to inhibit exhibitors: they steal, flagrantly, as a matter of business practice. Distributors can hire firms that specialize in spot-checking box-office tallies, but this is expensive and there is no guarantee that the employees of these firms are not in league with the thieves in the box office.

(2) **Theatre employees, particularly including theatre managers, steal from the theatre owners.** The classic method is to "palm" tickets. Tickets are taken from the customer and then resold; either the customer doesn't care that he hasn't received back a torn stub, or, in a more subtle variation, he gets one back—the theatre's half of somebody else's ticket. In this manner the kid who tears the tickets and the little old lady in

the box office can rip off a couple of hundred dollars a week.

The theatre manager gets his by playing the nice guy and letting the little old lady go home early on Friday and Saturday nights so she can baby-sit for her grandchildren. He then takes over the box office and stashes the receipts from a couple of heavy weekend showings into his pocket. In many parts of the country it's a tradition that the last showing on Saturday night belongs to the theatre manager. People who go to movies don't notice the numbers printed on the backs of their tickets; all the manager has to do is to sell seats from a ticket roll of his own, or from one not numbered sequentially with those previously sold. If he happens to own the theatre, he can remove the stubs later from the ticket-taker's box, and there will be no evidence against him. If he is an employee, there are other means at his disposal, including a split with his boss. Either way the filmmaker loses.

(3) **Exhibitors get kickbacks which represent additional forms of theft from distributors and producers.** They may force a distributor to place his advertising through an agency which they own, or with which they have an "arrangement." The agency gets a substantial reduction from newspapers based on line volume. The distributor is charged the normal rate, and the discount is divided by the agency and the exhibitor.

The exhibitor may also present the distributor with bills for various "expenses." Some pathetic arrangement of still photographs under glass will be billed as $1000 worth of "display." There will exist an official-looking receipt. Needless to say, most of this $1000 goes back into the exhibitor's pocket.

(4) **Exhibitors are notoriously late in paying film rentals.** It is common to wait weeks, months, and even years for payment. During this time the exhibitors have the interest-free use of your money to acquire land, build more theatres, and perpetuate their vicious practices.

(5) **Some exhibitors do not pay at all.** Naturally, after a while, people stop renting them films. In the meantime they make a quick killing, and when the possibilities are exhausted, sell off their theatres and go into something else.

(6) **Although it is against the law, certain major distribution companies seem to have a "lock" on certain theatres.** In New York, for example, where exhibition space is in short supply, and where there is great pressure for films to do well at the box office or else get thrown out of a theatre, illegal under-the-table agreements by which certain studios have what amounts to an unwritten lease on certain theatres are common and accepted practice. This affects the independent filmmaker whose picture is being distributed by a small company. He does not have a fair crack at the theatre of his choice, and may be forced to exhibit in a house entirely inappropriate to his film. The fact that this is contrary to the antitrust laws, and particularly to certain court decisions pertaining to the film industry, seems to bother no one.

(7) **Theatre owners constantly and knowingly abuse their customers.** In a particularly notorious case, a certain theatre in New York deliberately announced the starting time for a certain feature as thirty minutes before that feature was due to go on. The theatre

manager then arbitrarily decided that no one could enter the theatre until the previous show had let out. The purpose was to display a long line of ticket-holders to passersby and thus create word-of-mouth reports that the film was a hit.

Once he buys his ticket, the customer is abused in many and various ways. In New York one of the specialties is to set up a maze of ropes and pens outside the theatre. The ticket-buyer is lined up in these and then patrolled and abused by ushers who issue savage instructions about staying in line and moving along and stepping to the front and looking lively. On the Upper East Side of New York going to the movies is to experience the tactics of storm troopers.

Once he is inside the theatre, the movie-goer is subjected to dust and filth, debris under his seat and chewing gum on his armrests. In the huge theatres that specialize in long films with intermissions, it is common to find only one drinking fountain producing the merest trickle of water, hidden away down a steep flight of stairs or near the rest rooms, while a centrally located candy counter dispenses thirst-inducing orange drinks at inflated prices.

When the film finally begins, there is a lot of pretentious lowering and dimming of lights and opening and closing of curtains, designed to make it impossible to see the credits. Then there is static in the sound system, streaks and blotches on the print, missing frames, at least one projector out of focus, arcs burned so far down that the screen is not equally illuminated, and reel changeovers executed so badly that the audience's suspension of disbelief is regularly interrupted.

The irony is that every year the National Association of Theatre Owners holds a big convention during which they bemoan the shrinkage of the film audience, and blame filmmakers for creating poor "product."

*F*ailure

Sooner or later you will make a film that fails. It will not only fail at the box office and in the eyes of the critics, but it will also fail as a concept, as a work of art, and as a film. Failure may come about because your original concept was unworkable, inferior, and doomed. Even when your concept is good, the gulf between intention and final result is greater in film than in any other art form. The problems that arise between the time you get an idea and when you complete your first composite answer print are so many, so various, so unpredictable, and so often out of your control that failure at some point is almost inevitable.

How do you deal with failure? It is difficult to accept, particularly at the beginning of a career. The tendency is to go into a depression, to reconsider your ambitions, to question the premise upon which you have worked—that you have talent and the ability to make good films. There is also another question that obsesses filmmakers and which they rightly pose to themselves after a failure: whether filmmaking is really worth all the pain and anguish it seems to entail.

It is good to ask these questions, over and over, not only after a failure, but also after a success. They are endemic to the filmmaking profession, and unfortunately there are no satisfactory answers to them. But in regard to failure, there is something to be said for accepting it with pain, and then coming back to try again, invigorated by past misfortunes. It is the essence of filmmaking that one has ups and downs, that one fluctuates between exhilaration and despair. The film-maker should respond to failure the same way he responds to success: he neither quits on account of disaster nor rests on account of praise; he goes out and tries to make another film. There is an old saying in Hollywood: "You're only as good as your last picture," and it rightly implies the very callous truth that it is harder to make a comeback than a first effort. The authentic filmmaker, when he has failed, accepts this challenge and tries again, if only out of a stubborn love for film.

Film as Therapy

Film, because it is chic and glamorous and "now," has lately become a medium of therapy. There are people who believe that if children from deprived backgrounds could just get a camera and some film and go out and make a picture, this would serve their need for self-expression, become a therapeutic outlet for their fantasies, and correct psychological imbalance due to poor economic and social conditions. This idea seems predicated on the belief that because film plays such an important role in our cultural environment, self-expression in film comes naturally to young Americans.

The only real value of such films lies in providing interesting documentation of the psychology of the underprivileged, but more poignant documentation can be found in painting, poetry, short stories, and still photographs. The truth is that film is a very difficult medium with which to express oneself, it is expensive, and it is extremely awkward in the hands of beginners —something that is evident from any viewing of student films. The idea that film, because it is a mass medium, is accessible as a medium of mass expression, is one of the great hoaxes that has been foisted upon us, usually by radical-chic filmmakers wallowing in the luxury of a relieved social conscience because they manage to find the time to teach film to ghetto teenagers.

Film Festivals

Originally film festivals were occasions for filmmakers to get together, look at one another's work, fraternize, cross-fertilize, and if they were lucky, be honored by awards. Today they have become pseudo-cultural events, promoted by Chambers of Commerce to boost the local economy, or by people who wish to elevate their social status by connecting themselves with the chic and glamor of film. They have also become marketplaces where distributors and producers make deals, buy and sell "product," and vie for prizes with extraordinary crudeness.

For an unknown filmmaker with a small and modest effort in hand, film festivals, for all their faults, are good places to showcase his talent and test out his film on an audience. For these reasons, and because *some* festival directors are more interested in the artistic values of a picture than in its ability to please a crowd, the filmmaker should consider entering his work in a festival.

Some notes on the major festivals:

AMERICAN FILM FESTIVALS

The filmmaker's best chance is at a festival in his own country. There is no need to subtitle and no language problem with jurors, critics, and prospective distributors. Most important, it is much less expensive and complicated to enter a festival in the United States. There are six major American festivals.

(1) NEW YORK. Very elegant, very social, very important. Unfortunately there is not much room here for American films; the New York Film Festival has traditionally been a place to screen foreign pictures shown previously at foreign festivals. The purpose is to bring pictures of artistic importance to New York, and in this the New York Film Festival has succeeded admirably. One can fault the selection committee for a certain prejudice in favor of the French school (a bias derived from the pages of *Cahiers du Cinéma*), and also for some blatantly inconsistent choices such as *Bob & Carol & Ted & Alice*, clearly selected to broaden the festival's popular base. But there have been evenings at Lincoln Center when the very tough audience has been electrified by exciting new work, and for this we must be grateful. The New York Film Festival is well covered by important critics.

(2) SAN FRANCISCO. Much less successful and less interesting than New York, principally because the festival directors over the years have played a triple game: going for the usual arty stuff from Eastern Europe, favoring works of the political underground, and at the same time trying to corral Hollywood blockbusters. (Physical proximity has resulted in yearly overtures to Hollywood which have become all

the more frantic as the resistance from Southern California has stiffened.) The result is that the San Francisco Film Festival satisfies neither filmmakers nor audience, and has become a second-rate event, priding itself on such accomplishments as presenting the world premiere of *The Sergeant*. One plus: the authorities in San Francisco will look at and give consideration to off-beat works by unknowns.

(3) CHICAGO. Surprisingly good, and highly respected by some Europeans who consider it the one important and incorruptible American festival. Over the years Chicago has captured some excellent pictures which have somehow escaped the attention of the people in New York. They will look at works by people they do not know, and are eminently fair in their consideration, selection being based solely on artistic merit. Chicago gives prizes, and the Chicago film critics are very young, very bright, and responsive to works of quality.

(4) ATLANTA. Atlanta may be the Athens of the South, but the atmosphere of its festival is sleazy and hick town. Pretentious and empty avant-gardeism is as honored here as the most conventionally plotted and second-rate independent features. Atlanta charges high entrance fees and gives a prize called the Phoenix, which means nothing.

(5) ROCHESTER. This festival has just started out and it's still too early to tell whether it will survive. Because it is allied with the very fine Edinburgh Festival, the pictures are excellent and interesting. The question is: why Rochester? Nobody knows the answer, except that it has nothing to do with Eastman Kodak.

(6) DALLAS: It sounds awful: a film festival in America's City of Shame; screenings at the Bob Hope

Theatre at Southern Methodist University! Actually, it's interesting on several counts: it's the only festival in America restricted to American films; there is an honest attempt to create a rapprochement between Hollywood and the East Coast Underground; the selection committee is made up of distinguished critics. If this festival survives its first few years, it could turn into an important event.

EUROPEAN FESTIVALS

There are hundreds of festivals in Europe. The ones listed below are the major events.

(1) CANNES. For years the most famous film festival in the world, very commercial, very social, known for lavish parties, appearances by glamorous stars, rudeness by audiences, fights among jurors, and incredible wheeling and dealing at the Carleton Hotel. Some of the most interesting films are shown in the side events and critics' sections, and there is more going on here than one person can possibly absorb. An experience not to be missed, but that should be endured no more than once.

(2) VENICE. Second only to Cannes in fame, perhaps more elegant, and more oriented toward film-as-art. Many fine pictures have won awards here, and the same cannot be said for Cannes where the prize-giving has often been scandalous. Venice is becoming more political; it is still the principal showcase for the Italian directors; the city, itself, provides a setting equal in fantasy to anything you are likely to see on the screen.

(3) BERLIN. Interesting, tense, very political—the leftism prevailing at so many European festivals is

most pervasive here. More avant-garde than Cannes or Venice, always controversial, and definitely worth attending or entering.

(4) EDINBURGH. Sober, intelligent, in excellent taste, and a pleasure to attend.

(5) LONDON. Like New York it is a compilation festival, but unlike New York it sometimes sneaks in and out of town, unnoticed.

(6) Moscow. Held every other year, it is grandiose, fascinating, unlike any other festival in the world. Although extremely pro-Soviet in its bias, and somewhat provincial in its selections, it is a must for a filmmaker if he happens to be in Russia while it is going on. There is not a chance in the world that a small film will be accepted here.

(7) MANNHEIM. Youth-oriented, political, and of great interest to American filmmakers, to whom this festival has been very kind through the years.

(8) SAN SEBASTIAN, KARLOVY VARY, MAR DEL PLATO (in Argentina). These festivals are typical, although a cut above hundreds of others where Golden Doves, Eagles, Lions, Apollos, Crabs, and whatever else happens to have local significance are doled out by the truckload. There is a consistent mediocrity to most of these festivals in which big pictures are listed and don't arrive, big names promise to come and then don't show up, reservations and tickets are hopelessly snafued, juries are corrupt, prizes are worthless, and there is always a harried and well-meaning festival director running around trying to calm people's tempers. The problem is that the audiences in most of these places are not very interested in film. The three listed as examples all happen to be held at resorts, and this may constitute their very slight distinction over the many hundreds of others which are not.

Film Schools, Film Students, and Student Films

Just as most professional newspapermen didn't go to journalism school, most professional filmmakers don't have degrees in the art of the cinema. Part of the reason for this is that the breakthrough to film directing is not a formal process that comes out of years of study and a subsequent working one's way up through the ranks, and part is because the industry has traditionally resisted the film-school graduate on the grounds that anything he may have learned at school is irrelevant to the filmmaking process. Despite a great deal of talk about how times have changed, you don't see lots of talent scouts hanging around film-school campuses.

In the United States there are over fifty universities offering degrees in film; numerous film departments in colleges, art schools, and schools of architecture and design; a great number of fly-by-night academies of cinema; and three major centers for the study of filmmaking: the University of Southern California, the University of California at Los Angeles, and New York University. All three schools are excellent, and if it were possible to characterize them, one could say that N.Y.U. is more oriented toward a gritty documentary look and independent features, while the two California schools are more oriented toward a glossy, theatrical type of filmmaking and a career with the studios—doubtless because of their proximity to Hollywood.

In the rest of the world there are five major film schools: I.D.H.E.C. (Institut des Hautes Études Cinématographiques) in Paris, which is highly preferential toward French students and quite theoretical in its approach with lots of *explication du film*; the Centro Sperimentale di Cinematografia in Rome, which is an excellent practical school of production techniques oriented toward the theatrical film; and the three East European schools, in Prague, Warsaw, and Moscow. Prague and Warsaw are particularly fine, but, again, difficult for foreigners, and the Russian school, the least exciting of the three, is really a feeder for the state-controlled Soviet cinema industry.

The trouble with American film schools is that although the instruction is often very good, the facilities usually are not, and the opportunities to make films are very slim. Another trouble is the students.

There is something about film students today that is very discouraging. Film departments seem to attract all the lost souls in a university, and the talented and committed ones are a small minority in a sea of freaked-out, lost, and despondent souls who clutter up these departments and strain their limited facilities.

Film students tend to express themselves in a similar and banal fashion, along two equally dead-ended routes: the angry politicos with their films of protest, and the hippies with their films of fantasy. Both groups deal in stereotypes and clichés and most of their films are indistinguishable one from another.

The politicos are into the "revolution," which they usually and unintentionally depict as an adolescent farce. Protesting students run on screen from the left, and the fascist pig police run on from the right. They collide in the center of the screen in a brawl of nightsticks and blood, into which brawl is cut subliminal flash-frames of Robert Kennedy, Mick Jagger, the filmmaker's girl friend in the nude, and the filmmaker himself engaged in some feat of sexual overkill.

Meanwhile the speed freaks, acid heads, and freeze-dried love children present their weird filmic fantasies. In these one is likely to see a surrealistic drug trip, an incomprehensible series of juxtaposed counter-cultural motifs, or just a bunch of characters sitting around someplace "grooving."

Contrary to all the publicity about a great surge of filmmaking on the campus, and polls that tell us that 30 percent of all American undergraduates want to be film directors, one has only to go to a festival of the best student productions to come away discouraged and depressed. The truth is that most campus filmmaking reflects a terrible indulgence of kids who have no business being in the film medium. None of them want to be editors or cameramen or screenwriters; they all want to be directors, they all want glory, and they all say they are artists. Yet they are unwilling to pay the necessary dues or to acknowledge that excellence in film, as in any art, comes from years of hard work. They go into movie theatres, look at what's on the screen, sneer, complain, and tell you they can do better. They tell you that the system and the establishment are rotten (which is true), but then, by some peculiar logic of their own, they use this as an excuse not to struggle against them. Their most pathetic rejoinder to pleas that they go out and do some hard work is that they don't have time for that because they have to "express themselves."

"Well, man, tell us just what it is you want to express?"

This question is met with a blank and uncomprehending stare, as if it were impertinent. The important thing, one is supposed to surmise, is that they have very intense feelings that need an outlet, and these feelings can't be explained.

"OK, then, what makes you think they can be expressed in film?"

Another blank stare, and then a string of *non-sequiturs* about something very vague and ominous that will surely destroy the questioner and his terrible ilk, some frightening thing called "the revolution."

OK, one is sympathetic to tormented young people, and their need for an outlet. Paint a picture, make an earthwork, write a poem, tutor in the ghetto, hitchhike to Guatemala, do anything at all, but don't think you can work it out with film. Film is technical and its technique must be mastered; film is expensive and there is not enough money to pay for this kind of indulgence; and film is a medium of mass communication to which the private fantasy may be transferred only by a trained and committed artist.

Student films today are like student novels and short stories ten or fifteen years ago: filled with adolescent melancholy, self-indulgent, self-pitying, self-conscious, sensitive to the point of irritation, and amateurish. Everyone is entitled to an outlet, but fifteen years ago, when the student wrote his novel, it didn't cost anybody anything, and it didn't involve a lot of other people.

There are film students who will tell you with great pride how they walked off the set of their own student production because they couldn't get along with their student cameraman and their student actors. *Walked off their own set!* It is unbelievable, but one hears things like this from film students all the time. The director who walks off his own set doesn't deserve a second chance. His walking off doesn't prove his artistic incorruptibility. It proves that he is not, and never will be, a filmmaker.

One might well ask, "How do I know whether or not I have it to be a filmmaker?" A good question. The answer lies with the people who teach film. They should never encourage an individual who does not have talent, and, in this time when everyone wants to be a filmmaker, they should set extremely high standards for entry into their courses and carefully interview everyone who applies. Secondly, they should tell their students, day after day, year after year, about that old-fashioned thing called commitment, without which any artist is a mere dilettante. Thomas Mann defined the dilettante very well when he wrote that he was a man who made "the mistake of thinking that one may pluck a single leaf from the laurel tree of art without paying for it with his life." That is something every filmmaker knows.

Filmmaker, The

The concept of the filmmaker as a man who literally *makes* a film from beginning to end—who applies his talent and creativity to every phase of motion-picture production, selecting the material, developing the screenplay, choosing the cast and the key technicians, directing the shooting, and supervising the editing and completion—is easily grasped by the young. Unfortunately young people make the mistake of thinking that this concept is now generally accepted by the film industry. It is not.

Many people in the industry pay lip service to the

idea of "the filmmaker," but when conflicts arise, the people who finance pictures expect those they are paying to dance to their tune. In some cases, when the director is a "heavy" talent and highly "bankable," the financiers must, by contract, leave him alone. Still, there are very few American directors who have the right of "final cut" on their pictures—the ultimate legal authority to impose their vision upon their own work.*

In certain circles within the film industry, the idea of "the filmmaker" is very strongly resisted. In these circles the director is considered an item of "above the line"** talent, a man who is for hire, a man to whom a script or package is offered, with whom a fee is negotiated, who goes on the payroll as an employee, and into whose hands a picture is given for the vital and risky phase of shooting. In these same circles the real "picture maker" (as they like to call him) is the producer or head of the studio; these people believe that the ultimate creativity is performed by the man who controls and shapes a picture by hiring talent and applying it judiciously to his projects. Even very recently, some new, young, and self-styled "hip" production-distribution companies have emphatically restated this concept: if they don't like what the director presents to them, they will change it, with or without his help and consent. They have the same problem as the old studio moguls—they cannot accept the role of businessman and manager; they are obsessed with the idea that they are "showmen."

The concept of "the filmmaker" is, by its very nature,

* "Final cut" literally means that the edited or cut version of the director is final and cannot be altered without his consent.
** "Above the line" refers to the way film budgets are drawn: talent costs are listed "above the line" and technical labor and other production expenses are listed "below the line."

difficult to accept in a capitalist society. When it is accepted, it is only out of fear (when the old way of doing things has led to too many losses) or intimidation (under the duress of an important talent with a big box-office record). The idea of the financier calling the shots is much more basic to the American character than any concept of "the filmmaker." Thus the young filmmaker should be aware that the position to which he aspires is in constant jeopardy and that the struggle for artistic supremacy of the artist will always be the struggle of those who make films.

First Films

The purpose of making a first film is to insure the possibility of making a second. This is so obvious that it is frequently forgotten by young filmmakers who spend their time and money on various projects, all interesting in their own right, but irrelevant to the final objective of making theatrical features. If you want to make full-length fiction films that people will pay to see, then there is no point in creating animated shorts, abstract shorts, films made from animated still photographs, surrealistic fantasies, one-line and one-gag cinematic puns, films filled with special effects, or one-take, full-face, on-camera interviews. Such efforts may be extremely powerful, brilliantly conceived, cleverly cut, and they may reflect great technical virtuosity, but people in the business will qualify their admiration by asking two classic questions: can this filmmaker work with actors, and can he tell a story on film? For all the other benefits and pleasures that may accrue from these kinds of shorts, they do not answer either of the questions, and therefore, for the prospective maker of features, they are a waste of time.

There are a great many projects that can be achieved with a small amount of money and which can be presented in a format that demonstrates an ability to inspire a performance, construct a scene, and structure dramatic material. It's not necessary to go out and spend $25,000 making a featurette with music and fancy titles and big production values; with as little as $500 a young filmmaker can produce a brilliant and powerful scene between two people. For a little more he can make a ten-minute dramatic short, either as a story in itself, or in the form of a segment from a larger project (i.e., a feature).

The possibilities are endless, but the principle remains constant: if you want to work with the big screen, then everything you do, beginning with your earliest films, should be directed toward that end. Otherwise you may become diverted, and although you may pick up some prizes and get screened in museum auditoriums, the second film, and the third film, and ultimately, the first feature, will be no closer to realization.

Grandiosity

Grandiosity is a disease that has always afflicted filmmakers, and even in this age of the intimate and personal film, young filmmakers are by no means immune to it.

It's not that there is anything wrong with thinking big, or even with the idea of film as a vehicle for spectacle. But there is a tendency for things to get out of proportion when vast sums of money and vast filmic concepts are bandied about. When things do get out of proportion, either in relation to the worth of a particular project, or the value of a particular concept, or even in terms of what a sum of money could mean in some other area, there is disruption, and things can turn out very badly.

One trouble with grandiosity is that when huge sums are being expended, the very concept of "the film-maker" becomes lost. When this happens, much of the possibility of obtaining an artistic result is also lost. Huge enterprises require huge managements, and it is very difficult for a single person to give artistic unity to a film that costs $20,000,000 and in which the very logistics of production are so complicated that the production managers begin to take control.

An example of grandiosity deriving from a bad concept is the Soviet production of *War and Peace*. This film is reputed to have cost $100,000,000, and is thus the most expensive film ever made. The concept was to take one of the longest and greatest novels ever written and transform it into one of the longest and greatest films. The transformation did not work. *War and Peace* is a beautifully mounted production, and in terms of sheer spectacle, or, as they say, "production values," it is hard to imagine anything more lavish or in better taste. But *War and Peace* is a boring film; at its center it is dead; and the reason is that those responsible for the film completely misunderstood the nature of their material. The characters invented by

Tolstoy are warm, palpitating human beings; on the screen they are cold cardboard. The greatness of the novel lies not in the fact that it is long and epic, but in the intensity of the characterizations, the conflicts that the characters have with one another and within themselves. All this was sacrificed for the big scenes, with the curious result that the figures in the background seem more real than the foreground principals. Sergei Bondarchuk's film is at best cold and uninvolving, and at worst a scandalous extravagance for a nation that professes to be a People's Republic.

A very different example of grandiosity is Mike Nichols' production of *Catch-22*. Here the money has not been spent on production values. *Catch-22* does not look cheap, but it does not look any more expensive than many $3,000,000 wide-screen war films with airplanes and extras. The money, reportedly some $20,000,000, was spent in another way: first, on "above the line" costs (fees to the director, writer, performers, and producers, and the cost of the original property), and second, on time, on the months it took to shoot, on the care and control in setting up shots so that the director could execute his concept exactly as he harbored it in his mind. Here the grandiosity did not consist, as in *War and Peace*, in taking a great novel and transferring its most superficial aspect to the screen, but in taking an interesting but by no means sublime book and inflating it beyond any value it could possibly have, seeking to make something important out of something of medium consequence.

Catch-22 does not look lavish. In fact, some deliberate effort has been made to give it a modest look. The money, we are assured, was spent on the artistry. But that is just the problem. If *Catch-22* had cost $3,000,000, it would still be the same film—interesting, skilled, somewhat pretentious, not particularly memorable—but it would no longer be grandiose. Its grandiosity lies solely in the fact that its $20,000,000 worth of artistry does not add up to art. No one can place an absolute value on a work of art. A Rembrandt can be worth $500,000 or $5,000,000; it doesn't matter; its true value lies beyond money. But when a filmmaker spends $20,000,000 because he says he needs that much to make a work of art, and then presents us with a work that is merely artful, it is a scandalous extravagance. (It may also affect the credibility of other filmmakers with large and expensive projects, and in this sense, too, it is scandalous.)

It would be wrong to single out Bondarchuk and Nichols, as if their grandiose schemes were any worse than those of other filmmakers. George Stevens, for example, took a great event in human history, mounted it expensively and lavishly in a film called *The Greatest Story Ever Told*, and ended up trivializing it in the tradition of Cecil B. DeMille. *TORA, TORA, TORA* deals with the Japanese attack on Pearl Harbor with less emotional force than a cheap newsreel made in 1941 in which footage of the actual event and Roosevelt's speech to a joint session of Congress conjure up the full meaning and tragedy of December 7. And *Cleopatra* may be the worst of them all: without even the distinction of representing the corruption and misunderstanding of a great literary work, it is the product of Hollywood hacks and seems to have been created purely for the sake of being grandiose.

Grandiosity does not apply to every film that is big and expensive. *Gone with the Wind* is mythic, and its size and spectacle are in proportion to its purpose; *Around the World in 80 Days* gives pleasure on account of its bigness; *Lawrence of Arabia* is a rare example of art imposed upon spectacle. The problem, as has been said, lies in the sense of proportion. A film becomes grandiose when millions are spent on a misunderstanding, a rotten concept, to satisfy an ego, to do something that could be better and more powerfully expressed at a fraction of the cost, or because someone believes that large expenditures insure the importance of a film and a filmmaker.

Clearly one of the great attractions of the film medium is the opportunity it affords the filmmaker to create a universe, to build a world and people it with characters out of his imagination. There is a very great temptation to shoot a scene where a girl says goodbye to her boy friend, having in the background a thousand men marching off to war. The filmmaker may know that the scene could play effectively with the parting taking place in a grove of trees and the marching thousand implied by the sound track, but he wants to see those thousand men, his concept is that juxtaposition, and so he tries to shoot it that way. Perhaps he is right. The question is not whether the scene he wants to do is too big (although it may be impractical at a time when big budgets are very much against the trend of the industry), but rather whether the way he wants to do it is right or wrong for the film. If it's wrong and he does it, he is grandiose. If it's right and he does it, then he is thinking big.

Hit, The

The only reason a major studio ever finances a particular picture is because its management thinks that that picture will become a hit. The industry exists solely on account of hits. If there were no such thing, there would be no private money available for making films, and filmmakers would have to work on an extremely modest scale and under some system of subsidization.

The filmmaker, although not adverse to making hits, has other interests, among them the making of good films. That many good films lose money is a natural consequence of the well-known thesis that artistic quality is irrelevant to pleasing the audience; the two don't seem to be connected—they may coincide, and then again, they may not.

A man like Robert Bresson who has been making fine, austere, introspective films for nearly thirty years, without the slightest regard for the box office inspires admiration. His films seem almost contrived to displease the mass audience. But there are very few filmmakers with his kind of purity. Most filmmakers, in their hearts, want to hit it big, not necessarily for their own profit, but for that feeling of exhilaration that comes from knowing millions of people are lining up to see their work.

It has been said that the qualities that make a hit are mysterious and unfathomable; that if anyone knew the secret, he would be the richest man in the world; that financing pictures is like shooting dice, and that the picture business must be played like the stock market, on the basis of knowledge of the past, understanding of the market, and, in the final analysis, instinct.

It is this element of instinct (or "feel" or "touch") that is most talked about. It is generally believed that certain people have good instincts and others do not; that a few golden ones were born winners and the rest of humanity was born to lose. When the man who has been winning suddenly loses, as he inevitably must, people say he has "lost his touch." When he is doing well (successes, strangely, seem to come in series), they say he is "hot."

Actually, it's not very difficult to account for a hit, after the fact. As soon as a picture hits with the public, one can find a thousand reasons for its success. Many people attribute a hit to a "hot" filmmaker, one who, they believe, has an uncanny ability to please the public. This has resulted in the trend of banking on certain directors. Others claim that hits come out of a chemical reaction between story, actors, and director that ignites the work into something greater than the sum of its separate parts. The chemistry theory may account for the current interest in film packages.

A much more interesting theory, though perhaps too cerebral for application by most studio executives, is that *a picture becomes a hit when the fantasy it represents coincides with the needs of a particular segment of the audience at a particular time.* The man who makes the hit, then, feels the unconscious cravings of the public, and he invents and realizes a fantasy by which these unconscious cravings are fulfilled.

This theory has a number of interesting implications. The first is that the ability to know and fulfill the unconscious needs of people—to "resonate" with them—depends upon a deep and instinctive understanding of the audience. One cannot resonate with people one does not know. One cannot live in isolation, either in a cabin in the mountains, or in an office in Manhattan, or in splendor in Beverly Hills, and continue for very long to conceive of films that fulfill an audience.

The "resonator" is ahead of his audience; he knows in advance what they crave. Not only is he one of them, feeling their needs and discontents, but he also knows how these needs and discontents can be satisfied. Thus, being of them and ahead of them at the same time, he is in a very tenuous position. The second implication, then, is that the ability to resonate may be very short-lived.

The third implication is that the most important component of a hit is its story-concept. This is not to say that personnel are unimportant, but that excellence in choosing personnel is not enough. If one is interested in fulfilling an audience, the most important decision one makes is in choosing the right story and knowing the correct style in which it must be told; after that, the selection of director, cast, music, etc., will be obvious.

The fourth and final implication is that once a certain fantasy has fulfilled an audience, the territory it has covered is burned out—at least for a few years. Imitations of hits can make some money, but the imitations are never as successful as the original, because if the original fantasy has really hit the audience, then the need is fulfilled, and the imitation merely mops up the residue. This idea goes against the whole tradition of the industry, which is to look at the biggest hit of the moment, extract what seem to be its most attractive qualities, and weave these into a number of imitations. The current economic depression in Hollywood may be attributed in good part to the enormous success of *The Sound of Music*. Studios looked at the grosses on this picture and decided that expensively mounted film versions of Broadway musicals were gold mines. The result: about ten imitations which dropped dead and tied up so many millions of dollars that several of the studios lost their financial stability.

The theory of the hit as a product of fantasy fulfillment can be illustrated by the film *Easy Rider*. *Easy Rider* has been called a "sleeper," defined as a film which nobody expected to hit and which therefore appeared to be "sleeping." All big hits are "sleepers," because in fulfilling a previously unrecognized need, they are just that: i.e., unrecognizable in advance.

Easy Rider fulfilled a craving by a particular segment of the audience (alienated young Americans) for a certain way of life (free, cool, and adventurous) and, at the same time, articulated an apprehension about America (that it is evil) which had not previously been articulated on film. The moment it appeared, it was instantly recognized by millions of young people as certifying a certain fantasy and a certain truth they had come to hold. Before they saw *Easy Rider* few of them knew they wanted and believed these things; the instant they saw them on the screen, they knew that this was the way they felt.

Much has been written that is highly critical of the *Easy Rider* fantasy, particularly the dealing in cocaine which some intellectuals believe undermines the whole premise that its heroes are anticapitalistic and, therefore, "good." Thus, they say, *Easy Rider* is a swindle, and the audience has been "had." This kind of analysis is irrelevant because the question is not whether *Easy Rider* is consistent in what it seems to be saying, or whether its admiring audience has been duped; the question is whether the young, rightly or wrongly, felt fulfilled by it. The box office on *Easy Rider* proves they did.

The leaders of the film industry have looked at *Easy Rider* and have, as usual, made all the wrong deductions. They see that it is a low-budget picture, that it has to do with dope and motorcycles, that it presents an apocalyptic view of America, and that it was bought by the entire youth audience. Thus they have set out to imitate all these characteristics, believing that all films should be inexpensive, that all films should be youth films, and that all young people are interested in dope, motorcycles, and apocalypse. They have totally missed the point, which is that *Easy Rider* at a given moment fulfilled a certain segment of the audience; that the needs of the *Easy Rider* audience were changed the moment they walked out of the theatre; and that there are other audiences still to be satisfied. The lesson of a hit like *Easy Rider* is not to imitate it, but to realize that a particular territory has been used up and that it is time to move in another direction. The imitations of *Easy Rider* will do no better than the imitations of *The Sound of Music*, although, on account of their low budgets, they may lose a good deal less money.

The hits of the next few years will be made by people who have an instinct for what the public wants before the public knows it wants it, and, from time to time, each audience—the so-called youth audience of *Easy Rider*, the so-called family audience of *The Sound of Music*, the so-called schlock audiences of *Airport* and *Love Story*—will be fulfilled by works that will be called "sleepers."

Probably it is not possible to sit down and consciously analyze the needs of an audience and then set out coldly and methodically to fulfill them. One either knows and understands and resonates, or one does not. In the meantime the industry is so attached to the theory of imitation that the filmmaker may have to do a little dancing in this area, promising his prospective financiers that he is going to make another *Easy Rider* or another *Love Story* even if this is the furthest thing from his mind.

The eyes of studio executives will suddenly become unglazed when you mention your current project in the same breath with hits that have turned to gold. The more you are associated with films that have made money, the more welcome will be your ideas. As long as this is the way the studios want to shoot the dice, it is easy to play along, holding your cards close to your chest, knowing that any man who studies box-office figures only knows what the public is buying today, and that the new hits will always be forays into psychological territory previously unexplored.

Hollywood

As Detroit is to cars and Pittsburgh is to steel, so Hollywood is to film. Hollywood, or "the Coast," as it is often called, is the capital of the American film industry. Although it's no longer necessary to move to Los Angeles to work in film, and although films today are made everywhere in the world, Hollywood remains the center. Tattered, frayed, it is still the place where most production decisions are made, and it is still the home of the studios.

For the filmmaker driving around town and passing

the "dream factories" (Kremlinlike fortresses guarded by impenetrable security), there is a strange sensation: the knowledge that behind these walls are all the tools, all the talent, and all the money he needs to practice his profession, as well as all the venality, all the vulgarity, all the stupidity, and all the greed that have degraded the screen so many times. All the resources are there, a few feet away, waiting for him to mold them into film, and yet getting his hands on these resources is so difficult and entails such hassles that they might as well be on the moon.

The first thing the filmmaker must understand about Hollywood is that if he chooses to live there and fight the fight, he must submit to an environment that is among the worst and most destructive in the world. Los Angeles must be the vilest place man has ever built. It is, indeed, Plastic City, land of billboards and smog, freaked-out hippies and tar-coated beaches, unbreatheable air, vicious and unrelenting freeways, where the only protection against insanity is to take up an idiosyncratic life-style revolving around witchcraft, organic food, radical-chic, cars, ostentation, drugs, sado-masochistic orgies, or anything at all that can be used as insulation against the surrounding horror. One can fall into despair thinking about how this environment affects the sensibility needed to make good films. The gestalt of Hollywood—its endless vulgarity and its infinite corruption—seems contrived to make good work impossible; the miracle of Hollywood is that, despite itself, some good work does get produced. The only explanation is that in the immense concentration of resident actors, cameramen, writers, producers, and directors there exist some outstanding artists who have managed to maintain and even enlarge their gifts against incredible odds.

Buried in the enormous number of people who make

up the film industry—press agents and talent agents and publicists and bookkeepers and secretaries and management personnel—is a hard core of skilled craftsmen who represent Hollywood's principal contribution to film production. There are people there who can build a set, dress it, light it, put makeup on an actor, correct a film emulsion, mix a sound track, and perform the ten thousand other technical chores of filmmaking better than people anywhere else in the world. Their expertise, their craftsmanship, is the best there is, and it is at the disposal of anyone who can pay for it.

The problem with skills like these, however, is that they have very little to do with excellence in filmmaking. While Hollywood has spent years and millions cultivating technique, it has forgotten style. While it has learned how to manufacture a product, it has forgotten how to decide which products are worth manufacturing. It has attained knowledge without wisdom, skill without taste. Meanwhile a tiny and poorly equipped film industry in Czechoslovakia, without a tenth of Hollywood's expertise, has made films that have moved audiences.

It makes no difference to the Hollywood craftsman whether he is working on a third-rate television series or on an important work of art. He works for the money. When you approach a technician on a set and ask him how it's going, he won't tell you about the excitement or lack of excitement of the project, or the brilliance or lack of brilliance of the performances; he will tell you that there's lots of overtime or not much overtime, that a lot of guys are working or a lot of guys aren't.

This is the tragedy of Hollywood: that its people are so corrupted by money, and its expertise has been misapplied for so long, that the distinction between making good pictures and the condition of the film industry is no longer recognized. In Hollywood you can buy everything you need to put a fantasy onto celluloid; everything, that is, except what is most essential: you can't buy magic in Hollywood. The "dream factories" might as well be steel mills. Hollywood might as well be Pittsburgh. The spark is gone. The embers have died. For the filmmaker, Hollywood may be inevitable; it is, after all, still the place where most pictures are made. But the essence of Hollywood today is that no matter the ups and downs of its financial condition, as a place for the working artist it is dead.

Honest Count, An

Truthful financial statements from exhibitors, distributors, and production companies of moneys spent, moneys received, and moneys owed to you—in short, an "honest count" is something you don't get in the motion-picture business.

Improvisation

Improvisation, as a technique for working with actors in rehearsal, understanding a scene, and exploring a character, is one thing; improvisation on the screen is quite another. When it works, it is fascinating, and when it doesn't, which is most of the time, it represents a terrible self-indulgence on the part of the film-maker, and leads to boredom and disengagement by the audience.

There is a temptation for the filmmaker to approach a project with the idea that he will provide a scene outline to his actors, and let them "write" the dialogue. Some directors want to do this out of a genuine desire to achieve naturalness on the screen, and others because they are either too lazy or too inept to do the writing themselves. In either case, the approach is filled with dangers.

Scenes improvised by actors who know what they're doing can have about them a freshness and naturalness and truthfulness that is often lacking when scripted material is performed. But improvisation, even with experienced professionals, is always a crap shoot. A wrong move here, a mistake there, and the scene suddenly loses credibility and momentum; a remarkable moment achieved in one improvisation may not recur the next time around; what is fresh may quickly become mannered; what looks great when you're shooting may look awful when you're coolly judging it in the screening room; and, finally, improvisations are very often open-ended, wandering, unresolved exchanges that lack the cogency and thrust that film, with its very stringent problem of elapsed time, often demands.

The greatest danger of all, however, is that improvisations cannot be controlled. They get out of hand, not only in terms of length and thrust, but also because the actors may move and speak at unexpected moments. Then only multiple cameras or a documentary form of shooting can fully capture their performances, and the director loses the power to design his shots. Improvisation on film means ceding a great deal of control to a cameraman and allowing actors to impose their taste and ideas (without directorial restraint). The great dividend, when improvisation works, is the achievement of marvelous acting moments, but films which sacrifice imposed concept and story thrust to virtuoso acting are more gratifying to the actors involved than to anyone else.

Perhaps the best solution for the filmmaker who wants to use improvisation is to do what Brian De Palma and John Cassavetes have done: improvise scenes, tape-record them, transcribe them, and then use the improvised material to write or rewrite the original dialogue. This method gives the actors an opportunity to collaborate on choice of language, to experiment, and to search for new meanings, while at the same time the director maintains full control.

Juggling and Hustling

In the early stages of his career, a filmmaker is much like a carnival huckster, dancing down a tight-rope, thinking about things like the Sistine ceiling, juggling hand grenades, and trying to talk a great number of self-satisfied people into betting that he will reach the other side and catch a hen that lays golden eggs.

Juggling is a very important part of the filmmaker's life. He should have at least a half-dozen projects in motion at all times—treatments, scripts, proposals, and also ways of making a living. Most of these projects will slip out of his hands, but if there are enough of them in the air, then he may manage to catch one or two.

In *The Hustler* Paul Newman played a man who pretended to play mediocre pool in order to induce people who thought they played better pool to bet *against* him. Once the bets were down, he played pool to the limits of his great talent, and won. The young filmmaker must hustle in another way: he must induce people to bet *on* him, because he has inspired in them a hunch that he may earn them $1,000,000. When Paul Newman was found out, those whom he had hustled merely broke his thumbs. When the filmmaker fails to make a fortune for his backers, they withdraw their support and break his spirit.

Juniors and Heavies

If you work in film for very long, you will meet a great number of people. Some will become friends and some will become enemies; there will be people who will cheat you and people who will be straight with you; you will meet young people and old people, winners and losers; in short, people of every type. Of all the distinctions you must learn to make, the most important is the difference between a heavy and a junior, and, for that matter, between things in film that are heavy and things in film that are light. The importance of this distinction cannot be overestimated. It applies to everyone in film, from actors and agents to producers and directors, and to every aspect of film, from screenplays and packages to films themselves. It is a distinction that is partly, but not always, qualitative; that has something, but not everything, to do with achievement; that reflects both objective and subjective standards; that is important and unimportant, irrelevant and basic, all at the same time. The ability to make these distinctions cannot be taught; there simply comes a day when the recognition of what is heavy and what is light, who is heavy and who is junior, is plain and intuitive. The terms involved cannot be defined, but the following notes may serve as a guide for the reader who must, in the end, define them for himself:

(1) Heaviness and lightness are words that do not pertain to bulk or to physical weight, or, for that matter, to heavy-handedness or to a "light touch."

(2) Within a corporation, relative titles and positions on a company organization chart do not necessarily express relative degrees of heaviness. A heavy is a prime mover and he may or may not be the company president.

(3) A heavy gets things done. When he speaks, people listen. When he says he is going to do something, he does it. When a junior speaks, people begin to stare at the floor. When a junior says he is going to do something, you cannot be sure that he will.

(4) Heavies in the film business do not refer to somebody not present as the "boss," unless they are being deeply ironic. Although a heavy may be an employee, he is not supervised. He may be fired for making a mistake, but he is never called on the carpet.

(5) A heavy is decisive and gives you a straight yes or no answer, which is the most you can ask from anyone. A junior strings you along, interminably.

(6) When a heavy says "no" he means "no," and usually there are no further grounds for discussion. When a junior says "no" it doesn't mean anything except that at that particular moment he is feeling negative.

(7) Heavies say "no" with a smile, and kill you with a grin. Juniors like to stick in the knife, twist it in the wound, and then rub in some salt just to make sure it hurts. This gives juniors a satisfaction that heavies do not need, because being heavy is satisfaction enough for them.

(8) A heavy is not difficult to get to see, the first time around. A heavy returns your calls or else lets you know that in the future you had better speak to somebody else. A junior is very difficult to reach, and makes a point of not returning your calls.

(9) Heavies use juniors as messenger boys; juniors pretend they have messenger boys of their own.

(10) Heavies play their cards very close; juniors often say things they should not say, and don't know when they've tipped their hands.

(11) Heavies make mistakes, which they are happy to admit. Juniors are always right—at least according to them.

(12) Heavies are frequently ungraceful. They also tend to dress simply and without pretension. Juniors are mod and hip, and their grooming is contrived.

(13) A junior tells you that he "vetoed" a certain project; a heavy tells you that he talked it over with the boys and that "they" decided against it.

(14) Heavies are often impolite. This is not intentional; many of them are simply crude. When a junior is rude, it is usually with a purpose.

(15) Sometimes when you are in a meeting with a heavy, there is a long silence, a dead hole in the conversation. It may seem awkward to you, but it does not bother a heavy. A junior, on the other hand, will always try to fill a hole.

(16) A heavy is just as likely as a junior to cheat you, but he will do so on a much grander scale.

(17) Sexual orientation is irrelevant to heaviness.

(18) A heavy agent can put together a package very rapidly and sell it to a major studio with an apparent lack of effort. Junior agents set up meeting after meeting with juniors at various studios; half the time these meetings are cancelled, and on those rare occasions when they actually take place, there is a great deal of fast talk and no results.

(19) Women, of course, can be heavies. There are many, particularly among actresses. A common error is to confuse a woman who is a killer with a woman who is a heavy.

(20) Heavies, like certain *maîtres d'hôtel* in first-class dining rooms on transatlantic passenger liners, have seen a great deal of the world and are impressed by very little. Juniors are very easily impressed, especially by success.

(21) Heavies who are producers like to gamble. If you ask one why he took a certain chance, he is likely to say something about the hair sticking up on the back of his neck. Juniors hedge their bets, with this writer

and that writer, this star and that star. Juniors also tend to intellectualize their decisions.

(22) Heavies form the aristocracy of film. Their proportion to juniors is roughly that of one to a hundred.

(23) On many occasions it is fun to deal with juniors, but one must always remember that one is playing a game, and that nothing exists until it has been certified by a heavy.

(24) Juniors tend to be more charming than heavies. Needless to say, the last thing the filmmaker is interested in is charm.

(25) Many directors who have made a great number of interesting and successful films are not heavies. It is difficult to say why. Perhaps something that one cannot define is missing from their work. Elia Kazan is a heavy director, and Sidney Lumet is not.

(26) Perhaps the heaviest of all actors is John Wayne.

(27) Orson Welles and Marlon Brando are representative of a very rare breed who cannot be characterized as either heavies or juniors. In their work there are elements of both which commingle and cannot be unraveled.

(28) One of the many troubles with the television series *Bracken's World*, which dealt with the goings-on at a major Hollywood studio, was that one never saw a heavy. Bracken himself acted much too junior for a man with his apparent power, and his ace director, a character called Kevin Grant, was so junior, so feather-light, such a messenger boy, that it was impossible to imagine him directing anything except a series like *Bracken's World*.

(29) There is something about every film ever made by Stanley Kramer that has an aura of pseudo-heaviness. There is something about every film ever made by Stanley Kubrick that is indisputably heavy.

(30) The terms heavy and light do not pertain to tragedy or comedy. In fact, good comedies are always heavy.

(31) Everything about the film *Doctor Dolittle* is very light, and everything about the film *Dr. Strangelove* is very heavy. This may sum up the difference between these two "medical classics."

(32) It is *possible* for a hack to be a heavy. This implies that heaviness has more to do with the way a person sees himself than with anything he may do.

(33) In a performance, the quality that most pertains to heaviness is the actor's conviction.

(34) A heavy, like any big-time gambler, will take a loss with a shrug. A junior will brood upon one endlessly. A junior will also restage conversations in his mind, turning heroic phrases which did not occur to him when he was under pressure.

(35) Shots that confront scenes are heavy, and shots that caress scenes are light.

(36) Heaviness may have something to do with knowing who or what one is. Lightness seems to surround people and films that are seeking a category for themselves.

(37) The late David Selznick is often held up as a heavy because he was the producer of *Gone with the Wind*. However, there is something about the style of his famous and endless memoranda that smacks of

juniorism. This implies that heaviness may not be a permanent attribute, but something which comes and goes.

(38) It is very difficult for a film critic to be a heavy. It is impossible for a publicist or a press agent, no matter how spectacular, to be a heavy. There may be more heavy producers and promotors than there are heavy actors and directors.

(39) Heavies can fail, but only juniors can over-achieve. The words "heavy" and "overachieve" are contradictory terms and cannot be used together, because there is no limit to what a heavy can do.

(40) The statement "You are only as heavy as your last picture" is stupid.

(41) After a little exposure to people in the film business, one can make nearly instantaneous judgments about who is heavy and who is junior. These judgments may later prove to be incorrect, but generally speaking, one is more likely to overestimate a junior than to underestimate a heavy.

(42) One of the highest compliments that can befall a filmmaker is to have one or more recognized heavies say to him that his picture is good, and that it is moving. Other compliments, including the words "dazzling, stupendous, brilliant, devastating, best film I've seen all year, etc.," are strictly from the vocabularies of juniors.

(43) One of the surest signs that a person is a junior comes when he looks you straight in the eye and tells you that someone you never heard of is the greatest director in the world.

(44) The openings of films that are heavy seem to be energized by something that has gone on before the

film started; when such films are over, one feels that there is sufficient energy left to continue the story, if the filmmaker so desired. Light films, on the other hand, crank up while you look at them, and die when they are finished.

(45) It is necessary to understand the difference between juniors and heavies, and between light things and heavy things, because without this knowledge it is impossible to survive.

Laboratories

Most laboratories are huge bureaucratic institutions which couldn't care less about you and your low-budget film. Dealing with them is neither pleasant nor interesting, but, unfortunately, it is necessary.

Some notes on film labs:

(1) MONEY. If a lab is willing to extend you credit —in effect, loan you money by deferring the due dates on your bills and holding your negative as security— you should give it the highest consideration. Many labs will do this if you come on as a reputable person and if they believe in what you are doing. Of course, in the end, you must pay them back with interest, but there is not a bank in the world that will loan you money to make a picture, and the fact that many labs will do so, in the form of goods and services, is an amazing phenomenon.

Many young filmmakers believe that lab deferrals are a form of free money. They are very mistaken.

If you don't meet your commitments and pay your bills, they will seize your film, sell it (for scrap, if necessary), attach your property, and make sure you never get credit anywhere again. It is also very difficult to sell a film to a distributor that is encumbered by laboratory liens. In general, if you steal from a lab, you steal from yourself.

(2) CRAFTSMANSHIP. Sooner or later every lab, no matter how famous, screws up somebody's footage. This happens as a result of human or mechanical error. You minimize this risk when you go to a lab where craftsmanship is important. Labs that consistently do good work have good reputations and receive the loyal recommendations of their customers. Since craftsmanship is usually a by-product of morale, you can sense very quickly whether or not it exists in a certain lab when you talk to the section heads. If the chief of negative cutting or color printing sounds cavalier, you may want to go someplace else.

(3) A TROUBLESHOOTER. One can endlessly debate the pros and cons of the big lab versus the little lab; the fact is that no matter how large the lab, your problems will be solved if you have access to a troubleshooter. When you have a problem, the usual thing is for you to be shuttled from person to person, department to department, with everyone passing the buck and letting you know how little they care.

Try to find a lab where you can establish a relationship with a single person, whom you can call day or night, weekday or weekend, about anything that comes up, and whom you know will take responsibility for whatever happens and will do whatever has to be done. It doesn't matter how big the lab is; if you have someone like that, you'll get the same kind of service that is afforded to a company like United Artists.

(4) INTERPRETING WHAT A LAB TECHNICIAN SAYS. Inevitably there will come a time when you will be awakened by a phone call and informed by a deep and solemn voice that your negative is irreparably scratched. Try not to get too excited. Nine times out of ten it will be a false alarm, a tempest about something you can barely see.

Labs are staffed by old-timers who are obsessed with quality control and technical flawlessness—things which are irrelevant to low-budget filmmaking. They also are the type of people who want to make sure that you know that anything bad that happens is your fault. When they tell you that your footage looks bad because you haven't used enough fill light, they are really telling you that your footage looks bad because it doesn't look as if it was shot on a sound stage in Hollywood. When you've deliberately overexposed to achieve a special effect, they will be quick to inform you that your footage is uncorrectable. Obviously the only person in a position to judge footage is the filmmaker who shot it, but do not discourage them from sending you these emergency reports. If you know what you're doing, you'll be able to interpret what they say, and on those occasions when you're working with a bad camera, their solemn warnings may save you many hours of wasteful shooting.

(5) COMMUNICATING WITH LAB PERSONNEL. There are times when verbal communication with lab personnel becomes extremely difficult. You can tell a timer over and over again that you want a certain effect, and he will give you an answer print, over and over again, which you do not feel is acceptable. In such cases you should gently suggest sitting down with him and showing him what you want.

The people who work in labs are like industrial

workmen everywhere: they punch a time clock, they are into an adversary relationship with management, and they suffer from the dehumanization of the assembly line. Don't expect to be greeted with charm when you turn up with long hair and arms filled with film cans.

Management people also feel estranged from contemporary filmmakers. They yearn for the good old days when films were made by corporations and when orders for five hundred release prints were run-of-the-mill. If you are patient and compassionate, you can sometimes bridge these gaps, but you should never expect people who work in film labs to be passionate about film.

Low-Budget Feature, The

THE RELATIONSHIP BETWEEN BUDGET AND COMMERCIAL VALUE

When one begins to discuss the budgets of films, it is appropriate to examine some of the basic principles that apply to their commercial value. A film, for all practical purposes, has no tangible value. No matter how much it may have cost, its physical value is a few dollars' worth of silver particles suspended in emulsion and some perforated celluloid that can be sold to an editor for fill. In addition, a film, like a book, but unlike a painting, is not an object that has value on account of its rarity or uniqueness. It is nothing more than a series of images which when projected and accompanied by sound are resolved into a fantasy. The value of a fantasy in the marketplace is purely psychological; it is dependent upon the number of people who are willing to spend a very small sum to see it. If one person pays $3.00 to see a picture, it is worth $3.00, and if a million people want to see it, it is worth a million times more.

Since the value of movies is so dependent upon the whims of the public, the question arises as to why anyone should spend $10,000,000 to make a film that nobody may want to see, when he can spend $100,000 to make a film that everyone may want to see. Traditionally, the theory has been that "you have to spend money in order to make money," but some recent and spectacular examples of expensive films that have dropped dead and inexpensive films that have earned a fortune have caused a crisis in the film industry that has not yet been fully resolved.

The justifications for the very great disparity in film costs are extremely complex, but put in the simplest terms, the psychological appeal of certain types of pictures seems to be enhanced by large expenditures (i.e., fees to movie stars whom people wish to see; payments to extras and for elaborate sets which satisfy the public's desire for spectacle; and the expense of purchasing best-selling novels and hit plays whose titles are "pre-sold" and whose stories will entice the public into movie theatres), while the psychological appeal of other types of pictures seems to be enhanced by qualities that are relatively inexpensive (i.e., sincerity, emotional involvement, truthfulness, and other virtues in great public demand).

Of course, both types of pictures have made money and both types have lost money. The problem for the industry has been its frequent inability to distinguish between these two sets of values and to spend money accordingly. One constantly sees films like *The Only Game in Town*, basically an intimate story of two people in an apartment, overproduced at a reputed cost of $11,000,000, and films like *The Slaves,* which might have had a fighting chance as entertainment if it had been mounted on a lavish scale and turned into a spectacle.

This leads to the first, and perhaps most basic, premise of low-budget filmmaking: *a low-budget film should not be a miniature of an expensive film.* This means that a low-budget film that seeks the production values of an expensive film is doomed to be shabby, and there is nothing that turns people off as fast as large-scale production concepts cheaply executed, or a film which pretends to be something that it is not.

This may seem very obvious, but it is frequently forgotten by producers. Over and over again people have tried to produce stories on a low budget which needed expensive production to succeed. The man who makes a low-budget film must understand from the very beginning that he must renounce the use of stars and spectacle and reliance on literary properties, and that he must direct his efforts toward simplicity, uniqueness, and the use of unknown talent. With this approach, and with the knowledge that whatever crudeness that results may be turned into an artistic asset, he is in a position to compete commercially with any film of any budget.

The psychological values he is seeking are marketable, as long as he does not dilute them by half-baked attempts to achieve values that cannot be cheaply instilled. It is financially practical to make a feature film on a low budget if one's concept is amenable to a low cost; a story like *Nothing But A Man* is a low-budget story, but an epic about Ché Guevara is not.

LOW BUDGET DEFINED

The expression "low budget" is defined in different ways, depending from which echelon of the industry you happen to be speaking. At a major company "low budget" may mean anything that costs under $1,000,-000. At a smaller company it may mean something between a quarter of a million and $400,000. For the filmmaker who wants to make a feature and raise his money from private as opposed to corporate or professional sources, a realistic definition would be $100,-000 or less.

TWO APPROACHES TO
LOW-BUDGET PRODUCTION

There are two different ways to approach production at this price level. The first is to follow the example of American International Pictures and Roger Corman and shoot a feature very quickly—in from seven to ten days. This is the "quickie" approach, and its *ne plus ultra* is found in the methods of the makers of skin flicks who have been known to shoot a feature in a single day.

The essence of the "quickie" is that since one hires professionals and pays them professional wages, the money is burned up fast, and the result is a film that is made without much style in a straightforward and mechanical manner. Such films can be very successful on a commercial level, but they have nothing to do with art. The "quickie" approach applies best to motor-cycle, bikini beach, horror, and other camp genres, in which the entertainment value of the story, as opposed to the artistic value of its execution, is the saleable asset. (In such genres there is no audience expectation of artistic quality; in fact, these films work because slick shoddiness has become an accepted stylistic convention when applied to material of this type.)

The second approach is to take a very simple idea and execute it with great artistic authority, thus implementing the values of truth and involvement and style. Such a film cannot be made like a "quickie," in seven days and at a shooting ratio of three to one, but requires rehearsal, weeks of shooting, and the ability to shoot and reshoot a scene many times until it is satisfactory.

If one wishes to make a low-budget film with artistic merit, one is faced with the problem of utilizing a very small amount of working capital to buy time and raw stock. Certain items, like equipment rentals and processing, can only be purchased at fixed costs, so something else in the production budget has to be sacrificed, and that item is people. This leads to another very basic premise of the low-budget feature: *with limited financial resources, it is necessary to underpay labor in order to buy film and time.*

A PRODUCTION CONCEPT THAT IS CONTRARY TO ACCEPTED PRACTICE

To pay very little for labor is to produce against the most rigidly adhered-to practices of the industry. On a normally financed feature, the major costs are the "above the line" fees to talent (for story, screenplay, director, producer, and cast) and technical labor.

Everything else (raw stock, equipment, editing and completion expenses, etc.) constitutes a relatively small percentage of the budget.

The low-budget approach is precisely the opposite. The major items of cost are the *things* (film, equipment, processing, etc.) and the "above the line" fees and salaries of technical labor are reduced to a mere pittance.

The first person whose wages are sacrificed is the filmmaker. By writing his own original screenplay, directing, producing, and editing his own film, all for a bare subsistence wage, he is contributing a minimum of $100,000 worth of "above the line" services for practically nothing.

It immediately follows that the low-budget film that is not a "quickie" does not employ union labor. This is possible only because there exists today a large number of semi-trained, energetic young people who are desperate to work in film. Scorned by the unions, desirous of experience, they provide a degree of commitment unknown among union craftsmen. They will work long hours, day and night, weekends and holidays, for a subsistence wage, and their energy and enthusiasm make up for their lack of experience, especially if managed by a filmmaker and a cameraman who know what they are doing. Thus by paying six such people $100 a week instead of paying fifty union technicians $400 a week, the independent filmmaker reduces the costs of his production crew by a factor of thirty or to something like 3 percent of what a Hollywood producer must pay.

Because of the simplicity and modesty of his material, and the fact that style and theme and performance are the values being sought, any crudeness that may result will become an asset, and be accepted by the audience as the cachet of the filmmaker's good intentions.

Just as the crew must be nonunion, so the cast must be non-Screen Actors Guild. There are so many unrecognized and unknown actors of talent who are willing to make a financial sacrifice (who, in fact, make one every day when they work in places like Off-Broadway) and who want nothing more than to show what they can do in a quality film, that quality of performance need not be affected by lack of production funds.

Finally, by shooting on locations instead of on constructed sets, by scrounging props and costumes, working with little or no overhead, using second-hand cars and borrowing and hustling whatever he can, the filmmaker can continue to reduce costs and buy those two essential items: time and film.

A final note on this concept of production: Clearly one is playing upon the eagerness and energy of people in order to induce them to work at a wage lower than they deserve. One is, to put it very frankly, exploiting the fact that so many people want to work in film and there is very little work available. This kind of exploitation is morally tenable of one allows oneself to be exploited in turn. If people are willing to work hard so that you can make a good film, you owe it to them to make a film worthy of their effort. You also owe them a chance to participate on both an artistic and a financial level. Finally, in no case should you pay yourself a single cent more than you pay to the lowest man in your cast and crew.

ON A LOW-BUDGET INDEPENDENT
FEATURE THE FILMMAKER IS
ON THE LINE

When the filmmaker works in this manner, he is putting himself on the line in a way that very few directors ever do. He either has something to say and is able to get his cast and crew to help him say it, or he doesn't and he can't. There is no fancy art direction, no sensuous movie star, no pre-sold story, or anything else to help him through. If he is inept, nothing will redeem his film, because its values or lack of them are totally dependent upon his talent.

Many people have made low-budget films, and most of them have failed, both artistically and commercially. The low-budget independent feature is the greatest crap shoot there is, because when it works, the payoff, both artistic and financial, can be enormous, and when it fails, it is usually a total wipeout. A hundred-thousand-dollar loss by a filmmaker who has access to only $100,000 of capital is more disastrous than a $20,000,000 loss by a company like M-G-M; and a film that exposes its maker as a man without talent means his chances of making a second feature may be less than were his chances of making his first.

An optimistic note. The independently produced feature *Greetings!* was made with approximately $15,-000 of working capital and another $25,000 of credit; it was original in both content and style; its maker, Brian De Palma, became widely recognized as a young director of great talent; *Greetings!* has so far earned over $1,000,000 at the box office.

Luck

Never discount the element of luck in filmmaking. It can make the difference between a scene that works and a scene that doesn't. Often when viewing rushes you will see things you never knew were there: gestures and juxtapositions between actors; objects and shadows in the background; extraneous sounds emerging from the ambience of the location—any one of which may turn the scene around and make it play. Sometimes you work and work on a scene in a certain way and nothing happens; then there is an accident and suddenly it comes together.

Dennis Hopper has spoken with wonder about an occurrence when he was shooting in Peru. A scene was completed and an actor had just stepped out of frame; on a hunch Hopper switched focus and found, directly in front of the lens, the heads of some sheep which happened to be grazing in a field in the background. In the context of his story and his concept, this coincidence seemed a marvelous and appropriate way to end the scene, and yet it was totally unplanned and was purely a function of his luck.

A thousand mysterious things can happen on a production, and when they are positive, we speak of the "magic" of filmmaking. Of course, there are two kinds of luck: good and bad. The trick is to encourage the one and discourage the other. A good producer tries to organize his production well enough to foreclose bad luck and still leave enough room for flexibility so that any good luck that comes along can be exploited.

Luck is also an important element when you are raising money or trying to make a deal with a distributor. Frank Perry was in great despair while trying to raise the money for *David and Lisa*. At one point, when he was almost totally broke, someone offered to buy the screenplay. He didn't want to sell it, but at the time he didn't seem to have a choice. He made an appointment to close the deal, but the buyer didn't show up. This turned out to be an enormous stroke of luck because the next day he found a major investor and it suddenly became feasible to produce the film and direct it himself, with independent financing.

Major Companies

There are seven major film companies: Universal, Paramount, United Artists, M-G-M, Twentieth Century-Fox, Warner Bros., and Columbia. They are the principal sources of motion-picture financing, and they are also the major distribution companies. There has been much speculation that in future years film production will be financed in a new way from a great number of diverse sources, but despite these prognostications, it seems very likely that as long as films are made, there will be companies which specialize in their production, and these companies will be the majors.

Each of the majors has had its day of being the hottest and also the coldest among the seven. Each also has its own personality, its own special "feel." In no particular order, and with the understanding that these personalities are subject to change at the switch of a management, one can say of the majors that: one is run like a bank, another like a law firm, another like an advertising agency, another like the Pentagon, another like a feudal fief, another like a retail store, and the last like some sub-division of the Mafia. The filmmaker must understand the crypto-bankers, lawyers, hucksters, generals, dukes, merchants, and *mafiosi* who manage these companies. Unless he can speak their language and relate to their motivations, he runs the risk of cutting himself off from the primary sources of professional backing.

The first thing he should know about the majors is that they are in business for only one reason: to make money. He will often hear this objective softened when someone says, "We want to make good pictures, because good pictures make money." Of course, this is nonsense. No matter how good a picture may be, if it does not make money, it is not good for a major company.

Yet such a statement implies the strange nature of the majors: they employ people, sometimes in very high positions, who often lose sight of the company's prime objective and who pretend, even to themselves, that their first interest is in the art of the cinema. Thus the filmmaker, when he approaches a major, must convince the people he is addressing that his project will make money without ever stating it in such crude terms. He must present his proposal in such a way that his listeners are able to make the leap to dollar signs without his help. Otherwise, if he comes in and says, "Now this is how we're going to make a million dollars," they will think him either a charlatan or lacking in what they believe should be the artist's disinterestedness in profit. They want the filmmaker both ways, and he, unfortunately must oblige.

The second thing the filmmaker should know is that a major company's interest in his talent has a great deal to do with how little it will cost. There is a tendency on the part of the young filmmaker to become very arrogant about his "hotness" and youth, to think that because he is finally dealing with a major, he is in a position to hold a gun to the company's head and demand a huge fee—the kind of fee he has been reading about for years in articles about Mike Nichols. This is not true. Every film is a gamble, and when the film is being directed by an inexperienced young man, the odds against the gambler go up. The only way this effect can be neutralized is to cut down on the cost of the investment. The minute the young filmmaker begins to get expensive is the minute he enters a disadvantageous competition with the big names and dependable giants who have attained bankability. The young filmmaker should therefore understand that what he has to offer a major company is the talent to turn a film into a hit, and a relatively low fee for that service.

Third, the filmmaker should understand something very essential about a major company's vulnerability: if it were possible to obtain sufficient money-making product without having to finance productions, most majors would abandon the film production business and concentrate their attention on distribution. The reason for this is that it is much easier to evaluate the money-making potential of a picture when it is finished and on the screen and its total cost is definitely known than when it is a screenplay, a cast list, a budget, and some vague and inexpressible directorial concept.

There are men in the majors who love the crap shoot of film production and whose speciality is making judgments on just such flimsy evidence. But the more sober members of top management, particularly in the conglomerates which now control three of the majors* (and which may, very soon, end up controlling them all), know that this is an insane way to do business. Therefore it is absolutely incumbent upon the filmmaker to present himself as a reliable man. The "mad genius" approach may get him through several echelons, but when he reaches the top where the final decisions are made, he must act like a person who is sympathetic to the needs of the stockholders of a large corporation. Otherwise he may find himself in the position of a small-scale Orson Welles—a man whom everyone knows has talent, but whom very few businessmen can bring themselves to trust.

The dilemma of the majors has its ironic overtones. It is said, for example, that a hard-pressed Paramount tried to unload *Catch-22* on other distribution companies at its original cost. Paramount was reputedly in a financial squeeze at the time and needed the cash. Although a great many people who looked at *Catch-22* believed that it was a film of great merit, apparently no one thought it was worth what it had cost. Even if this story is apocryphal, it serves to illustrate a point: there is no doubt that the companies that turned down *Catch-22* in its completed form would have snapped it up if it had been offered in the form of the package that Paramount had originally bought: i.e., with Mike Nichols as director, etc.

This speculation implies that the majors are schizophrenic; they like to gamble and are afraid to gamble

* Kinney now controls Warner Bros.; Gulf & Western controls Paramount; Transamerica controls United Artists.

at the same time. The only way the filmmaker can cope with this is to become schizophrenic himself: to play various roles with various executives, to play the businessman without looking like a businessman, and to play the artist without overplaying. If the filmmaker succeeds in these roles and manages to soothe fears and calm anxieties, the majors may find him sufficiently interesting to grant him the temporary use of their money. If this happens, he should never forget that in their eyes he is a tool being used to manufacture a product, and that while he may be looking for a way to express himself with film, they are looking for a way to turn a profit.

Matching and Continuity

It should no longer be necessary to discuss matching and continuity as if these two things still constituted an aesthetic issue. Over the last decade enough films without conventional shot-matching and that smoothness of flow that is called continuity have been made and accepted by the audience to suggest that anyone who harps upon this subject is flogging a dead horse. Nevertheless, there are still a great number of people working in film who were brought up in the tradition that every sequence must be "cutable" in the classic, nonobtrusive, smooth-flowing sense of the word, and that props and cigarettes and food stains and positions of feet must be carefully and obsessively matched in order for the artificial convention of the cut not to disturb the viewer.

There is the legendary assistant director who says,

"Watch out, Mr. Fellini, you have just crossed over one hundred and eighty degrees!" and the script clerk who says, "My God! The flower pot is turned around, the rose petals are now facing the fireplace!" These types love to hold up productions and bore filmmakers, and when their admonitions are disregarded, they can be heard muttering words like "incompetent" and "doesn't know what he's doing."

Mostly they are laughable but they can have an insidious effect upon a young filmmaker who, after attracting some attention with a small production, finds himself on a Hollywood sound stage directing a major feature. Suddenly he is surrounded by an army of technicians who pride themselves on their expertise, and who are waiting to pounce on his most superficial mistakes in order to prove their indispensability. The young filmmaker's free-flowing, anarchic style is suddenly inhibited because these self-appointed heavies keep approaching him and telling him that he is not shooting enough "protection" and that no one will be able to cut his picture because everything is unmatched. They will enjoy keeping him waiting for hours in the afternoon before he can complete a scene he had begun that morning, while they correct the shadows that are now askew because the sun has moved.

The danger is that this kind of harassment (a thinly disguised form of hostility) will intimidate the filmmaker. It's all nonsense and part of a conspiracy to let the young filmmaker know that he is just a "punk" and has "a lot to learn." The best way to deal with it is to listen carefully to the assistant director, nod, and then tell him to get you a cup of coffee.

Message Films

Bob Dylan: "There are no messages . . ."

Miscellany

(1) NEPOTISM. The vast number of brothers, fathers and sons, fathers-in-law and sons-in-law, and other nepotistic combinations gives the film business a quaint provincial flavor which contrasts nicely with its pretensions of sophistication.

(2) RESHOOTING. There is a curious syndrome in the "big time": once a picture has wrapped principal photography, it is locked up and there is no going back. One young director who is hip to this, and is best left unnamed, makes it a practice everytime he shoots to leave out an essential shot. This forces the studio to approve a quick reshoot, at which time he grabs whatever material he needs, based on an analysis of his rough-cut.

(3) "I LIKE TO GET INVOLVED." These words, coming from the mouth of a studio production chief or an executive producer, may be the most ominous words a filmmaker ever hears.

(4) "I COULD HAVE BEEN SOMEBODY." That's what Marlon Brando says in *On the Waterfront* when he accuses his brother of having sold him out. Once a filmmaker's earning power reaches a certain plateau,

he inevitably becomes surrounded by people who see him as a property for their own enrichment, and who couldn't care less about his artistic needs. Since the whole point of being bankable is that one can do what one wants, it is very dumb to allow oneself to be manipulated into using this position merely to acquire wealth. It is the filmmaker's task to resist those who would have him sell out, so that he never has to say to anyone (wife, agent, etc.) in a self-pitying whine "I could have been somebody."

(5) THE MYSTIQUE OF THE MIX. There are filmmakers who make a mystique out of mixing the sound tracks for their films. They build up overrich textures, laying in track after track, and then waste hours striving for an ideal balance that is going to be imperceptible in a theatre. They do this because they want to give their pictures that "famous [insert the filmmaker's name] sound."

The only intelligent way to handle a mix is to collaborate with a good mixer, stay with him to keep him straight, and interfere only to give artistic guidance. Filmmakers who think they are technical wizards because they have just acquired a new hi-fi, and who try to elevate their role in a mix to the level of an artist engaged in a great creative act, are the laughingstock of sound engineers and a ludicrous sight to everyone else.

For all the talk about sound as a personal signature, there is only one filmmaker whose tracks are consistently brilliant: Orson Welles.

(6) BUDGETS. A lot of people have trouble making up accurate budgets because they go about it in the wrong way. They begin with a certain figure in their minds, and they approach the budget with the object of making all items add up to that predetermined total.

The only intelligent way to make up a budget is to approach it organically and build it from the inside after having determined a production concept and having accurately estimated the number of days it will take to shoot the picture.

(7) SOUND MEN. Good sound men tend to have a spaced-out look: they make contact with the world through a pair of earphones.

Bad sound taken by inept sound men has, unfortunately, become the signature of the low-budget film. If your sound man thinks it is sufficient to record by sticking a shot-gun mike into the faces of your actors, he is not ready for a feature.

(8) STARS. To paraphrase F. Scott Fitzgerald: let me tell you about movie stars; they are different from you and me. Stars are freaks—extraordinary human beings with a magical ability to project their attractiveness via the motion-picture screen. Because they are extraordinary, they are usually very interesting people, and also very difficult to love.

There are stars of the stage who never become stars of the screen because they lack some mysterious X-factor that is peculiar to the magnified image. There are many false stars, better described as "producers' stars." A star cannot be "created"; stardom is achieved only with the consent of the public, who know a star when they see one.

Some movie stars live on a scale so lavish as not to be believed. Stars deserve all the luxury they can afford: time after time they have created the box office for films whose only merits were their performances.

There is a certain type of star who deals in power plays of such heaviness that a young filmmaker can be chewed up for breakfast every morning on the set without ever knowing what has happened.

(9) SHOOTING. The making of a motion picture is an irrational enterprise, of which the shooting phase is the most psychotic. Only someone who has been through it can know the kind of madness and pressures that surround a director working on a set, and how this irrationality can combust into an artistic result.

(10) FILM LAWYERS. Unlike agents, they do not usually work on a percentage basis. It is therefore in their interest to "churn" a problem and build up the hourly costs. The thing to look for in a lawyer, aside from competence, is a sense of proportion. It can easily cost $5000 in legal fees to negotiate a deal that falls through, and which, even if it were made, would not have been worth this kind of expense.

(11) PUBLICISTS AND PRESS AGENTS. They have no shame. They degrade the art of film and they trivialize life by reducing it to chatter.

(12) ZOOM LENSES. These are invariably overused by young filmmakers who like to think of them as low-cost substitutes for a dolly.

Without doubt, the "smash zoom" is the most tawdry effect in the cinema.

(13) LOCATIONS. Filmmakers who pick out clever locations to stage scenes (i.e., in front of a lion's cage at the zoo, in the back of an auction house, etc.) usually can't resist foregrounding the location in order to rub the eyes of the audience into the ambience. This is unfortunate because it is always more tantalizing to use a background as a background, and, in effect, throw it away.

One good thing about locations that are difficult because they are small and without wild-walls and catwalks is that they force cameramen to come up with lighting that looks real. There is nothing so stupid as to go out on location and then light as if one were on a studio set.

(14) PROPS AND WARDROBE. On a low-budget film, a single exemplary prop that costs only a few dollars can achieve the same effect (i.e., certifying the reality of a set) as the Herculean efforts and enormous expenditures of a big-time Hollywood production designer. The same applies to wardrobe: some cheap store-bought clothes can be more effective than anything a professional costume designer can provide. The trick is to know which props and which clothes to buy; but that is what low-budget filmmaking is all about.

(15) MULTIPLE CAMERAS. In cases where a director wants to work fast and capture a sense of spontaneity, multiple cameras can be a good solution. Richard Lester uses them, and operates one himself, because he likes to view his material through ground-glass, flickered by a whirling shutter. Multiple cameras, however, are not a good tool for classicists because their presence tends to make shooting anarchical.

(16) WEATHER. Surely the filmmaker is like a god, in the sense that he creates a universe, but it is a symptom of pathological megalomania when he shouts at the heavens with raised fists, demanding changes in the weather. There are filmmakers who do this because, after years of blowing up bridges, derailing trains, burning churches, and slaughtering whole armies, something snaps in their minds. When the cosmic forces that control the weather refuse to comply to the filmmaker's demands, he is humbled by the recognition that he is only a man. This is the only good effect of the unpredictability of weather *vis-à-vis* motion-picture work.

(17) MONEY. One never wants to blow an interest-

ing deal by asking for too much, but one should always remember that the more people have to pay for a filmmaker's services, the more they value him as a person. When a filmmaker is paid very little he is apt to be abused; when he is paid a lot he is apt to be treated very well, despite what might have been a rough negotiation over his fee.

(18) MOGULS. Old-timers speak nostalgically about the days of the moguls (Louis Mayer, Harry Cohn, etc.) who, they say, may have been tyrants, but at least loved the movies. These grand old fellows are favorably compared to the new breed of "accountants" and "Ivy Leaguers" who now control the business and who are accused of being heartless and without a passion for film. Young people who become sufficiently intrigued by these assertions to read biographies of moguls find therein substantial reasons for wanting to resign from the human race.

(19) TO SAVE THE WORLD. It is interesting that producers who are out to save the world by making pictures with important social themes usually end up at the conclusion of these "idealistic" ventures with a couple of million dollars in their pockets.

(20) BERGMAN AND BERTOLUCCI. In a book in which the intention was to avoid a discussion of particular filmmakers, several names have come up because they exemplified certain points. This being the case, two additional names must be mentioned.

In Hollywood they refer to Ingmar Bergman with scorn as "that Swedish director who gets all the good notices but whose pictures never make any money." How little they know! Of all living filmmakers, Bergman may be the one who leads the most ideal existence. He lives and works the way an artist of the cinema should, with a company of devoted and talented collaborators, with access to whatever funds he needs to put his visions upon the screen, free from the interference of fools, the degradation of media-hype, and the exhaustion that comes from having to hustle projects among studios. He is totally and austerely committed to his work, and his pictures are consistently brilliant, highly personal and intense expressions. When one looks at the manner of his existence, one cannot help but feel sickened by the shabbiness that surrounds the life of the American filmmaker and the shallowness that seems to be his destiny.

As for Bernardo Bertolucci, they've barely heard of him in Hollywood, despite the fact that he may be the only exception since Orson Welles to the proposition that there cannot be a prodigy of the cinema. It is too early to say whether he will achieve greatness, but his gifts are remarkable and his films are electrifying. *Before The Revolution* is the finest first film since *Citizen Kane*. *The Conformist* is a masterpiece. It contains a scene in which two killings take place in the snow off a mountain road that employs so many levels of irony and parody and that is conceived and executed with such dazzling artistry as to suggest that he may become the Vladimir Nabokov of the movies.

Moment, The

A "moment" in film takes place when one or more actors achieves something so truthful and so profound that we, in the audience, are deeply moved. This rarely happens, and when it does, it is memorable. A "moment" may occur in a love scene or in a scene of confrontation or when a single actor is alone on the screen or when a pair of actors are in the middle of a crowd. It may be verbal or nonverbal, may last a few minutes or be over in a second. In a "moment" a character or a situation is so fully and profoundly illuminated that words cannot describe the endless ramifications of what has happened. In a "moment" there is a total sharing of emotion between characters and audience—a oneness that cracks the barrier between viewers and screen.

To mention just a few familiar examples: there occurs a "moment" of transcendent illumination in Elia Kazan's *On the Waterfront* when Marlon Brando and Rod Steiger are talking in the back of a taxicab; in the final minute of Federico Fellini's *La Strada* when Anthony Quinn weeps; in Joshua Logan's *Picnic* when William Holden and Kim Novak first dance; in Arthur Penn's *Bonnie and Clyde* when Warren Beatty chases Faye Dunaway through the corn; and in the final frozen frame of François Truffaut's *The 400 Blows*.

One could name many more examples; the effect is a familiar one and each lover of films has his own preferred list.

The problem with "moments" is that they cannot be contrived. There is no use in the filmmaker telling his actors, "I want this instant to be a 'moment.' I want you to work here for a 'moment.'" All he can do is put the necessary components together—place the right scene in the right part of the story, choose the right location, select the right performers, and perhaps most important, create the right mood on the set. Then he can only hope that everything will come together and that a miracle will occur. A "moment" cannot be forced; it either happens or it does not. It is a product of luck and chemistry and coincidence.

There is a great danger when a filmmaker consciously seeks out opportunities to create "moments": he is apt to push too hard and get something contrived, a pseudo-"moment" that is repugnant because it parodies the truth. This happens frequently to directors whose reputations are built on their achievements with actors. They begin to parody their best early work with rash and unsuccessful attempts to make "moments" happen. The later work of Elia Kazan seems to suffer from this problem. And the director who may be guilty of having contrived the greatest number of false "moments" is Michelangelo Antonioni. His films are filled with vast and interminable silences, mysterious interstices in which we are obliged to look for meaning and illumination, but in which we rarely find anything but a fashionable nihilism.

Music

Decisions regarding music are so important to the success or failure of a feature film that the filmmaker must never delegate the responsibility for making them to anyone else. The questions of, first, whether or not music should be used, and second, if there is to be music, exactly where it should occur and how it should sound, are so crucial that the filmmaker who defers them to a "music expert" might as well let someone else do his own final casting; he is evading one of his prime responsibilities, risking the ruination of his work, and if the result is unfortunate, he has no one to blame but himself.

Music, when it is well chosen, has a great effect upon the emotional impact of a picture. It is impossible to recall *La Strada* without remembering its haunting theme; Gillo Pontecorvo wrote his own score for *The Battle of Algiers* and his music works in perfect unison with his directorial concept; the music of *Midnight Cowboy* is so much a part of the film that it is inseparable from it; the use of the "Zarathustra" theme in *2001* has a great deal to do with the impact of its key shots; and *Casablanca* without "As Time Goes By" is unimaginable.

On the other hand, David Lean's *Ryan's Daughter* was so overscored by Maurice Jarre that the music pointed up the greatest fault of the picture: its grandiosity, "bigness" imposed on intimate material. John Frankenheimer's *I Walk the Line* was badly marred by the songs of Johnny Cash, songs which may have had merit in themselves, but when applied to this film, cheapened its austere purity. Only the great pictorial strengths of Alfred Hitchcock have redeemed his pictures from their bland studio scores, and as for the application of Handel's "Hallelujah Chorus" to the raising of Lazarus scene in *The Greatest Story Ever Told*—what can one say except that it was unmoving and embarrassing?

Fortunately the days when a love scene had to be scored with violins are now past, but the filmmaker must still fight endless battles with producers or studio production chiefs who cannot abide a "hole" in a sound track, or who want a hit tune to open a picture, or who insist on using talent signed by a subsidiary record company on every film released by their studio.

There was a time when every French New Wave

director slapped some baroque music or some Mozart onto his picture and let it go at that. Now, in America, we may have gotten to the point where every filmmaker scores his picture with music provided by a rock band. Both approaches are as silly as the old Hollywood way of always employing a big orchestral sound with lots of strings. The fallacy here, as in so many areas where the industry makes mistakes, is the imposition of something that has become fashionable upon material which it may or may not suit.

The latest fashion may be to open a film without any music at all, to roll credits over silence, or heavy breathing, or the twittering of insects, in order to assure the audience that they are about to see something *very important*. This is sometimes effective, but it can also become as pretentious as the use of clashing swords and heraldic insignia to open pictures about British history, strong-willed kings, troubled queens, and influential Archbishops of Canterbury.

One could go on and on with a list of films which have been well served and badly served by their music and the tendencies underlying bad choices. Too often a filmmaker may be excellent in all respects except musical taste. Or he may be in such a hurry to get on to his next project that he leaves decisions regarding music to other people. Or he may simply be too exhausted to endure a round of fights and hassles in an area that has traditionally been under the producer's control. Whatever the reasons, young filmmakers should know that it is a requirement of their profession that they acquire taste in music, that they carefully audition both melodies and arrangements of any music proposed for their films, and that they never renounce their veto over music, no matter how "heavy" the opposition may be.

Myths

Among young filmmakers certain myths are repeated over and over until they acquire the status of eternal verities. Here are a few that need to be punctured:

(1) "They'll 'fix it' in the lab." If your cameraman tells you this as you view his badly exposed and out-of-focus footage, he may be ready for firing. The lab will not "fix it"; the lab will *try* to "fix it." Overexposed and out-of-focus footage cannot be "fixed." If it has been shot correctly, there is a lot the lab can do, with timing and color correction, that will help a film, but it cannot make bad stuff look good.

(2) "We'll 'fix it' in the mix." The mix is the worst time to "fix" anything. At more than $100 an hour, it is not the place to make changes and suddenly discover you need a new transfer and that you forgot a loop. Low-budget features have abruptly gone over budget in mixing sessions that took five days when they should have taken two. An editor who goes into a mix unprepared, with bad tracks and bad cue sheets, is a dangerous man.

(3) "We'll get our money back on the college circuit." You may get exposure at colleges, but not too much money. A few distributors are just beginning to figure out how to reach this audience where it is alleged there is so much money to be made. In the meantime get over the illusion that the money is going

to roll in when you set up a projector in a student union and put an ad in the campus newspaper. You can make a fortune if you happen to have a print of *Citizen Kane*. Otherwise, don't count on it.

(4) **"If we get to rough-cut, someone will give us the money for completion."** There are several hundred features still in rough-cut awaiting that mysterious "someone" with the completion money.

(5) **"If we make a good film, we're sure to get distribution."** Wrong. You'll get distribution only if distributors think your film is commercial. This has nothing to do with whether or not your film is good.

(6). **"I'll shoot on weekends and all my friends will work for nothing."** Want to lose some friends? People don't like to work for nothing. They will work for starvation wages but not for nothing. Sooner or later they'll begin to ask themselves, "Why am I knocking myself out so that this guy can play director?" By the third weekend all the love is gone, and you'll have to suspend production.

(7) **"I'll make a short to showcase my talent."** It may work and it may not. There are a great number of people who have made interesting shorts, to which prospective financiers have reacted with a "so what?" Shorts are exceedingly difficult to sell, there is no viable way to distribute them, and they take a great deal of effort to make which might better be applied to a low-budget feature. This is not to suggest that shorts should not be made (since, as a matter of fact, there is no better way to learn filmmaking) but that their value, as showcases, is minimal.

(8) "I'm twenty-one, I just got out of film school, I won an award in a student film competition, and I'm ready for a feature." This is possible, but hardly likely, since the average age of a filmmaker making his first feature is thirty. Before one is ready to take this step there are a great number of things that must be proved, and a great number of dues that must be paid. Of all the myths, the young filmmaker's over-evaluation of himself may be the most dangerous, because it can lead to the kind of frustrations that make life very painful.

New York

Eddie Anderson, the narrator/antihero of Elia Kazan's novel *The Arrangement*, says at one point that he would rather be the manager of a Chock Full O'Nuts coffee shop in New York than the chief of a movie studio in Hollywood, the implication being that in the first instance his life would be charged with electricity, and in the second, mired in blandness.

For the committed young filmmaker, struggling for recognition and a chance to work, the choice of where to live comes down to Hollywood or New York. Both are nasty, tormented towns where the air is foul and the residents seem to live on the edge of a massive nervous breakdown. Yet they are the two centers for filmmaking in America, Hollywood having the edge in quantity of production, facilities, and technical skills, and New York leading in the size of its talent pool, particularly in the areas of acting and writing.

For the filmmaker who has to make a choice, the main considerations may be his own temperament and where he feels most at home. One thing, however, must be said for New York: for all its brashness, the incredible rudeness of its people, the unbearable pressures of its competitiveness, it provides more contact with the full range of human experience, a more intense clash of ideas, and a greater sense of aliveness than any other city in the world. For these reasons it provides young filmmakers with a stimulation that is conducive to good work. Although life in New York is less easy than in Los Angeles (there is less sunshine, fewer nice guys, and everything costs a little bit more), for those who can bear the strain, it may be the only place to live.

Nonactor, The

It goes without saying that to use nonactors in important roles in expensive films is to take a great chance. One often meets people who have a natural quality that is striking and attractive—who seem to be "natural actors." The temptation to use them is very great, particularly if a sense of naturalness is important to the concept of a film. Robert Bresson has been doing it for years, with remarkable results; so has Pier Paolo Pasolini, Satyajit Ray, Peter Watkins in *The War Game*, and the great master, Vittorio De Sica, who achieved such profound and moving performances in *Shoeshine* and *The Bicycle Thief*. Recently Gillo Pontecorvo used nonactors to great effect in *The Battle of Algiers*, but when he pitted an unknown illiterate against Marlon Brando in *Burn!* he was somewhat less successful.

The use of nonactors is an important subject with endless ramifications: when it works well it can produce great truthfulness and realism in performances, and an almost effortless style; at its worst it looks stilted, wooden, and unnatural. Clearly one does not use a nonactor to play a part suited to the theatricality of a George C. Scott, a Richard Boone, or a Yul Brynner—men who specialize in bravura character acting. On the other hand, it is doubtful that any member of the Screen Actors Guild could have done better than Chief Dan George in Arthur Penn's *Little Big Man.*

A general principle that applies to the use of nonactors is that they should not be required to play roles that are not close to their own lives. It follows that when one casts a nonactor, one begins the search in the place where the fictional character, if he really existed, would be likely to be found.

Directing nonactors takes great patience and great skill in handling people. The filmmaker who uses them must be prepared to waste film and to reshoot scenes many times, particularly in the early stages when the nonactor has problems of self-confidence and a fear of and unfamiliarity with the camera.

Nonactors cannot be rushed, and they must have total confidence in their director. The filmmaker, in turn, must be highly sensitive to the first signs that a nonactor is becoming terrified, and must move quickly and decisively to calm such terror. Terror, either of failure, or of the intimidating mechanisms of film production, or of the attention that is being lavished upon him, is the common affliction of the nonactor. When he is terrified, he forgets everything his director has told him; he forgets his lines and he freezes up. When this happens, one might as well stop shooting for the rest of the day because the chances of obtaining usable footage are slight.

There are many ways of dealing with nonactors. Robert Bresson is famous for turning them into marionettes, holding all the strings in his own hand. He dictates their every look and gesture, gives them precise readings for every line, shoots innumerable takes, and totally imposes his preconceptions. Other directors play a loose game with nonactors, searching for their exceptional qualities, seeking to use them for what they are inside rather than for the way they look or dress.

Whatever approach the filmmaker takes, he is faced, in the end, with the basic problem of directing: he must get people to give him what he wants. With professional actors he has a common vocabulary, he can depend upon a technical foundation and also upon a commitment to the profession of acting. When he works with nonactors he must deal with them on their own terms, as he would with people in everyday life from whom he wants something special. He must extend himself much further than with professional actors, and he must devote a good part of his time to relieving their self-consciousness.

The filmmaker must realize that the great difference between a professional and a gifted amateur is in the area of consistency. With a professional one can always depend upon a certain level of performance. A gifted amateur may be capable of great emotional heights, and also, within the same take, of great inauthenticity. This brings up the contradiction that is inherent in the use of the nonactor: the filmmaker wants the nonactor to be himself, and at the same time to pretend to be someone else. Even when the character being played is very close to the character of the non-actor, there is an element of "pretending" that cannot be dispensed with; inconsistency arises when the tension between "being oneself" and "pretending to be someone else" forces the nonactor to "act" beyond his unschooled abilities. When this happens, there is a crisis that can threaten the success of a production.

An interesting compromise, employed by several directors, is to use nonactors in small subordinate roles where they can provide a certain "richness" to a film, and where, if they do not work out, it is a relatively inexpensive matter to reshoot with someone else. Michael Ritchie did this in *Downhill Racer* and he achieved some excellent results without risking the total budget of his picture. Such a compromise is not the cop-out it may seem. Working with nonactors is a speciality, and failure is not uncommon. The young filmmaker may have enough problems simply dealing with his own insecurity and fright; to compound these by taking on the difficult role of reassuring nonactors may be to risk professional suicide.

Nudie Films

Nudie films, nudie-cuties, stag films, skin flicks, beavers, sexploitation films—whatever one chooses to call them, there is hardly an ambitious filmmaker who has not, in some moment of desperation, thought that they might provide an answer to his needs. A curious and shabby film by Fred Baker entitled *Events* deals, in the words of its advertisements, with "a young filmmaker, Ryan, who wants to make his own film, but who in order to raise money must first make some stag films. . . ."

There are certain things that "Ryan" and other young filmmakers who are similarly tempted should know:

(1) The people who back stag films don't like to turn them over to bright young directors because the whole point of producing stag films is to make them quick and dirty. Filmmakers are committed to care in their work and care costs money. Also, artistic camera angles and authentic performances won't bring one additional middle-aged gentleman into the theatre.

(2) When one works at a level and on a project beneath one's ability, one is apt to fall flat on one's face. When one is contemptuous of one's work, one is apt to fail at it. The same goes for literary types who think they can make millions of dollars by writing like Jacqueline Susann—without her very special mentality and utter confidence in the merits of her work, they haven't got a chance.

(3) The man who directs a stag film never makes more than a pittance. The hungry young filmmaker might do better running an elevator for a week. The only person who ever sees any profits is the producer who backs the production. And usually he likes to do his own directing, because it saves him a hundred bucks and gives him a chance to meet exciting young "actresses."

If, after you have grasped these points, you still want to make a nudie-cutie, then by all means go ahead. Who knows? You may end up with a huge contract from Twentieth Century-Fox and the commission to shoot a sequel to *Beyond the Valley of the Dolls.*

Packages

To form a package—that is, to put together an attractive combination of original property, screenplay, and commitments from a director and one or more stars—is the best method for laying a costly project on a major studio. In effect, the packager (who is usually an agent, but who can also be a producer or a filmmaker) presents his prospective backers with an assortment of goodies too tasty to resist. When you send around a screenplay you never know who is going to read it. It may go to someone in the story department who is just out of Vassar, or it may go to the president of the company; in either case it is subject to instant dismissal. When you send around a package that includes one or more bankable heavies, attention will be paid.

Packages are good for everyone. Agents increase their equity in a production by packaging it from among their own clients. Unknown filmmakers get consideration when they are packaged with recognizable stars. Lazy people at studios are saved a lot of work, and top management has an easier time imagining the outcome of a package than of a project that is merely in the screenplay stage. And, finally, there is something called a "packaging fee" which is of considerable interest to whomever it is paid.

The young filmmaker should, therefore, try to package his ideas, making them more attractive to major sources of backing. A good role may attract a star, who may, in turn, attract funds for production. The one danger is that the filmmaker may find himself forced out of the very package he created. "Sure, kid," someone will say, "we like your script and we like Paul Newman, too, but we don't know anything about you. Tell you what, though. We'll give you twenty-five grand, make you associate producer, and bring in Arthur Hiller."

This is the moment when the men are separated from the boys. If your script is good enough, and the star really wants to do it, you may be able to call the bluff. It is more likely, however, that when you turn down the counter-offer you will get that peculiar smile reserved for minor-league players who are trying to bat in the majors, followed by the kindly suggestion that you take your idea around to whatever studio is known at that moment as the House of Schlock.

Paying One's Dues

Success, "making it," recognition, are aims that have become unfashionable among the young. To want something too much is to be "uncool," and to be obsessed with one's work is to betray a single-mindedness many believe is "antilife." But in film, unlike any other art form, success *must* be achieved, because unless you are successful, you cannot work. An unsuccessful filmmaker sits around and thinks up ideas; only a successful filmmaker puts his ideas on the screen. As abhorrent and distasteful as the idea of "making it" may be, the filmmaker must know, and must remind himself again and again, that "making it" is essential.

To some people success comes very easily. They make a picture and they are instantly recognized. Such people are a golden few. For the average filmmaker, success comes only after a long struggle, after he goes through a process called "paying one's dues."

The word "dues" implies that there is some sort of club which filmmakers aspire to enter. In a sense this is true. The people who make features number only a few hundred, and the exclusivity of their profession has about it the aura of a club. There are many people knocking at the door, submitting applications, begging, even demanding admission. The membership roll is very small and the dues that must be paid are very high.

Paying dues means surviving put-downs, eking out a living, learning a craft, undergoing failure, trying to raise money, and numerous other painful experiences. Paying dues may mean sweeping a studio floor even though you have a *summa cum laude* degree in philosophy, or driving a cab to pay your rent. It means putting your work up on the screen and letting other people abuse you for it; being savaged by agents, producers, friends, family, and prospective backers, and still, through it all, knowing what you want, persisting, and coming back for more.

Paying dues means being willing to make great sacrifices in your personal life. It means knowing that your difficulties are uninteresting to other people; that no one cares how hard you struggled to make a film, what blood you lost and what tears you shed; that the only important thing is the final result reflected off a screen; and that self-pity is a worthless emotion.

If you go into film with a serious intention, you will

never sneer at "making it," and you will know that whatever pain you may suffer will not guarantee success. You will be quick to admit to having an obsession, and you will be willing to pay dues, no matter how high. This *willingness* to pay dues may be the least expensive payment you will ever have to make, because 99 percent of your competition will never appreciate the need for this willingness, and will rapidly drop away from the line at the clubhouse door.

Peaking Out

There is a phenomenon that is common to many filmmakers, including some of the best who have ever worked with the big screen: after making a certain number of good pictures, they peak out. Their talent becomes exhausted; their later films are pale imitations of earlier work; their efforts seem to lack inspiration; one detects the beginnings of self-parody, mechanicalism, a reliance on mannerisms, an inability to choose good material, the loss of taste, tendencies toward pyrotechnical effects at the expense of truth, and predilections for performances that are hyped up as opposed to performances that are rooted in conviction.

The list of symptoms is endless, and the disease is common to creative artists in all fields. (It is universal among performing artists, but that's another subject.) What may be unique is the speed with which the disease strikes at filmmakers, the relatively short span of their most fruitful years, and the rapidity with which they go into decline.

One can speculate about the causes of this phenomenon: filmmakers often isolate themselves from reality when they achieve great success, and that isolation may undermine their creative faculties; the inflation of a filmmaker's sense of self-importance can distort his ability to criticize himself; he may become worn down by the endless struggles of making pictures; the constant pressure to maintain his position can force him to go for box-office success at the expense of artistic self-fulfillment; the attainment of wealth, fame, and power may corrupt his vision; he may become surrounded by yes-men, receive too much unwarranted praise, allow his personal life and his celebrity to distract from an earlier commitment to work.

Aside from identifying the problem and speculating on its causes, one can do little more than warn the prospective filmmaker that if he does make the breakthrough, his professional life may be subject to this kind of destruction. The young filmmaker must remind himself, without being prematurely tragic, that the possibility of peaking out too early is very real, and that the best defense against it is to maintain one's sanity even if that means making fewer pictures and renouncing some of the accouterments of success.

Pauline Kael has written that Jean Renoir "is the only proof that it is possible to be great and sane in movies." Renoir may be the closest thing we have to a Shakespeare of the cinema, the only man who has ever worked in film whose every picture is touched by genius. Like Shakespeare, when he threw away his magic wand and retired to the country, there is in Jean Renoir a seeming lack of discontent. This is so moving because it is so rarely found in a contemporary artist.

Power

Power is so basic to filmmaking that its pursuit, attainment, use, and misuse are among the most characteristic phenomena of the filmmaker's life.

The making of a picture is fraught with struggles for power. Power plays between director and actor, actor and actor, cameraman and sound man, producer and director, writer and director, filmmaker and financier, are so frequent that a good part of the filmmaker's time is spent resolving power conflicts and maintaining his ability to work in the face of numerous attempted insurgencies and *coups d'état*. To make films is to get other people to do what one wants; the principal tool one uses is the power of authority; the filmmaker's authority is under constant attack; the greater the erosion of that authority (power), the less his chance of success.

The pursuit of power is the principal motivation in the filmmaker's professional life because his ability to realize his fantasies has everything to do with his ability to find backing for his projects, and that ability is contingent on his commercial, artistic, and personal power within the industry.

To make fiction films is to exert enormous power: to construct buildings, to people a set, to impose a vision, and to manipulate characters. To make films is to usurp the power of God: to create a universe of one's own design.

Then there is the power of the screen itself: the power to move people, to make them laugh and weep, to mold their opinions and influence their lives, to imprint images upon their minds with the intensity of a brand.

The man who does not understand the dynamics of power, the levers and buttons by which it is attained, held, and used, cannot succeed in the filmmaking profession. Successful filmmakers wear many disguises, but there is not a single one who does not possess a will to power, and there are very few who remember the valid truism that power corrupts.

Pretension

Pretension—making claim to undeserved distinction, raising big issues and then failing to deal wth them, coming on very serious and then trivializing important themes—is a booby trap into which American filmmakers seem particularly prone to fall.

Pretension often goes hand in hand with grandiosity (as, for example, in *Catch-22*), but there are pictures with modest production values and production costs which are nevertheless extremely pretentious. *Medium Cool* is an exciting work, but its pretension is so great that it undermines all the positive values in the picture. Not only does *Medium Cool* presume to tell us what is wrong with America, and weave in and out of a pseudo-profound discussion of the nature of film and the ambiguous polarity of illusion and reality, but it also exploits the political dilemma of the protestors at the 1968 Democratic Convention and uses their bloody struggles in the streets as the background (!) for an innocuous story about a mother's search for her lost or runaway son. This commingling of documentary truth and trite fiction degrades the importance of the former and points up the banality of the latter.

One does not pick on *Medium Cool* because its pretension is so much greater than that of other films (the first prize for pretension must go to Stanley Kramer), but because its pretension is so destructive of its other beautifully achieved effects. It offers a highly illuminating example of the dangers that arise when a filmmaker sets out to save the world.

At present young American filmmakers are an extremely politicized group, who must be particularly vigilant about the problems of pretension. If one's goal is to illuminate human experience and make statements on pressing social concerns, one is more likely to succeed by intense particularization of one's themes than by overt and redundant generalization. *Five Easy Pieces* may say more about America and the way we live than *Medium Cool*, and it is certainly more enjoyable. Finally, the American film audience is getting very turned off by preachments from the screen, and pretentious films are dropping dead at an increasing rate.

Producers

Many filmmakers act as their own producers, but there are some who prefer to work with a partner, either because they don't wish to be bothered with the business and organizational aspects of production, or because the partner contributes something they cannot secure for themselves.

Some notes on producers:

(1) **The first and most essential requirement of a producer is that he be able to obtain money to pay the costs of production.** It does not matter whether it is his own money, money that he raises from private sources, or money that he obtains by making a deal with a professional source—if he can get you the money you need to make your film, then almost anything else he does, no matter how stupid or bothersome, is forgivable. There are producers who are geniuses at organizing and administering a film production, but who can't raise two cents; they are less desirable than an incompetent who can raise $100,000.

(2) **Trouble arises between a producer and a director when the producer tires of his role as a businessman and begins to think of himself as an artist.** When this happens, the producer becomes just another source of hassles for the filmmaker, and more hassles are what the filmmaker does not need. Some very productive producer-director relationships have broken up over this point. Either the producer comes to think that while he does all the work, the director has all the fun; or he becomes jealous of the glory that accrues to a director when a film is successful; or he begins to think that he is talented and creative and should be making films himself. When this happens, intelligent partners recognize the problem and part amiably. However, there are many sick partnerships in which struggles for power burn up a great deal of energy that might be better applied to the making of films. A producer-director relationship is a very delicate thing, and only people who are sensitive to each other and mature in their dealings can outlast the pressures that tend to tear it apart.

(3) **There is a tendency for a producer to exert himself more strongly after the completion of photography than before or during shooting.** The period after shooting is dangerous for a director, because it is then that tendencies toward dominance, which may have been latent in the producer's psyche, begin to emerge with greater and greater force. Many producers think, without any justification, that they are brilliant editors. They begin to insist on changes in the rough-cut and upon a certain type of music, and they tend to oversupervise recording sessions and come back from screenings with lengthy lists of trivial notes. The psychology of this kind of behavior is very easy to understand: most producers are not creative in an imaginative sense; that is, they are not able to stage scenes or create something out of nothing. But once material has been shot, and the need for imaginative creativity is ended, a new and different sort of creativity comes into play. This is critical creativity, revolving around adjusting, polishing, adding, subtracting, and supplementing, and it is an area in which producers feel very much at home. As long as the filmmaker understands this phenomenon and how it represents the frustration of a person who lacks a creative imagination, he will be on guard against the kindly producer who becomes a monster once the footage is in the can.

(4) **Great producers are a rare breed; like great agents, they are in short supply.** The reason for this is that it is now fashionable to be contemptuous of business, and to insist on artistic outlets for "self-expression." The words "I'd like to make a few suggestions" can signify the calm before the storm. No matter how humbly this statement is made, its true meaning cannot be known until the "creative needs"

of the speaker are fully evaluatea. If the filmmaker can find a producer who loves producing, who does not have pretensions to being an artist, who accepts his responsibilities of the partnership, and whose suggestions are not consistently horrendous, he has found a treasure of great value. That such people are rare is the reason so many filmmakers have been forced to produce their own pictures.

Production Managers

Along with the cameraman, the production manager is the most important member of the production crew. A good production manager—one who really *manages*, makes arrangements, handles money, organizes the crew, and keeps everybody happy—is indispensable, and a bad one is ruinous. Many a low-budget film has been abandoned halfway through shooting because the production manager was incompetent or dishonest. On the other hand, many low-budget films were completed only because the production manager was a miraculous hustler who took a small amount of money and stretched it a long way.

Some ideal, but rarely found, qualities in a production manager:

(1) **He should be able to do the impossible.** No matter what you want, a great production manager gets it for you. A helicopter in Nebraska, lobster pots in the middle of the desert, permission to shoot in the White House, closing off Central Park in New York— it doesn't make any difference to him. He delivers it to you, and all he asks in return is a mild "thank you."

(2) He should be anal-compulsive. A good production manager does not swagger around and exhibit a great deal of personal style. He rarely sleeps, and whenever you see him his face is creased with determination and his body is dripping with sweat. He is obsessed with saving money, getting receipts and releases, and keeping track of every cent entrusted to his care. He has a neurotic compulsion to bring the film in under budget, without, of course, compromising any of its artistic values. He is uptight about time and possesses two wrist watches which he constantly cross-checks. He wears both a belt and suspenders, and has a cover location ready whenever a primary location falls through. He is a walking weather bureau, a great friend of the police, and has an uncanny ability to arrive in a town where he has never been and within days to discover and tap every local source of human and electrical power.

(3) He should be an eternal optimist and receptive to abuse. When you and everyone else on the production are exhausted and depressed, the production manager is the one who pops in and reminds you that "we got to do the rain sequence at 2 A.M." When you unjustly accuse him of screwing up, he does not resent your imperious tone, but is motivated to even greater efforts.

Because these are unbearable and inhuman qualities, the production manager is apt to be disliked. This is all right because it gives everyone on the production a focus for their gripes. On location, where the local scene is boring, the food and accommodations lousy, and everyone is getting very abrasive, the production manager acts as the company whipping boy and thereby serves a therapeutic function. The cast and crew sit around and talk endlessly about what an inhuman monster he is, and then, after the last shot of the film, they pick him up and throw him mightily into a nearby lake.

Within a couple of weeks after the end of shooting, members of the crew will come around to the cutting room and tell you that the production manager isn't really such a bad guy. In fact, it seems he's been writing this script. . . .

If he's a good production manager, the script is going to be terrible.

Raising Money

There is an analogy (not to be stretched too far) between a junkie with a hundred-dollar-a-day habit and a filmmaker who wants to make a film. Both need money desperately, and both spend a great deal of their time devising ways of getting it. The junkie becomes an appliance thief, and also deals in junk; against incredible odds he somehow manages to raise enough cash to survive. His life, however, becomes a nightmare; no matter what he does, no matter how much he steals and hustles and cons, every morning he wakes up with the same need, and every day of his life is a struggle of Sisyphean proportions. For the junkie there are only two possible solutions: he must either find a cure for his habit, or face an early and brutal death.

The filmmaker faces a dilemma *vis-à-vis* money

which, though less dramatic and apocalyptic than the junkie's, is, nevertheless, as never-ending and urgent. Once he commits himself to film—once he catches the germ and contracts the disease—most of his problems revolve around money. If he cannot solve these problems, then he must either give up as a filmmaker, thus committing a kind of spiritual suicide, or else lower his ambitions and thereby, in a sense, die a little inside.

The conclusion to be drawn by anyone who wants to make films is that he *must* get money, he *must* find enough, somewhere, somehow, to pay for the breakthrough that leads to professional financing. No matter that he is an artist and not an entrepreneur, that it is against his nature to become a money-raiser, that he finds money-raising degrading—he must do it or he cannot work, and if he cannot work, then he is a filmmaker only in name.

Some notes on raising money:

(1) **The best way to raise money is to find someone else to do it for you.** This is the best way, because you only have to convince one person of your merits, needs, and ability to earn back an investment, and then he does all the rest. The difficulty is finding such a person. You are looking for a partner with access to money and the push and the drive to get it. There are plenty of people who will make a few calls on your behalf, but who will get turned off very fast after a few refusals. A good money-raising partner wants to make the film as much as the filmmaker, and is one of those rare people who never gives up. Finding such a person may be harder than raising the money yourself, but if you are lucky and do find him, you are in an enviable position.

(2) **The first person you must turn to is yourself.** Of course, if you haven't any money, this is academic. Incredibly though, there are people who do have money, and say they want to make films, but who think that they should not be expected to invest in their own projects. The trick, they say, is to get other people to invest; this, they say, is what it's all about. Such a position is really untenable. If a person is unwilling to invest in himself, it is absurd for him to expect anyone else to take the risk. If you really want to make a feature, you should be prepared to invest every cent you have in the project, even if it means mortgaging your house and selling your wife's engagement ring. Such actions endow your pitch with the cachet of commitment and may attract the kind of people who are interested in a man willing to gamble everything on his own talent. On the other hand, if you prefer to keep your personal funds in stocks and bonds and real estate, then you don't deserve to make a feature film.

(3) **The next place you should turn is to your family and your friends.** The logic of this is obvious: your family and your friends are the people who should know you best and who should have the greatest reason to believe in you; if you cannot get money from them, then it is highly unlikely you will be able to get it from a studio interested solely in profits or from an investor with whom you do not have a personal relationship.

Despite the logic of going to family and friends, a surprising number of people balk at the idea. After living off their family for years, after accepting food and clothing and tuition and an allowance, they say they are unable to bring themselves to ask for more.

One can only reply that this is a psychological hang-up that is easily overcome if one is sufficiently committed to making a film.

As for friends, people say they don't want to exploit them. As long as you think of an investment in your film as a form of exploitation, you will never be able to raise a cent. It all comes down to one's belief in oneself. It is possible to ask for assistance in a way that is not degrading and that does not make people despise you. You have to use psychology, and you have to pick your people with care, but there is nothing undignified about turning over every stone for the means to create a work of art. The potential of your project may attract a certain type of person—perhaps your father, perhaps your cousin, perhaps your oldest friend—whose own life lacks the excitement and aura of art. Such people experience a legitimate kind of vicarious fulfillment when they invest in a film, and it is not exploitative to play upon this feeling. And, then, even if your family and friends do not invest, they may start you along a chain of people which may in time lead to someone who will. This, really, is the only way to find money: by being passed along from person to person until you get lucky.

(4) **A person who invests in a film does so for three reasons: he is interested in a film investment; he is interested in your specific project; and he is interested in you (i.e., he believes you can bring it off).** An interest in any one of these may provide sufficient grounds for following up and trying to create interest in the other two.

There is such a thing as a professional theatrical investor—a man who from time to time puts money into theatrical ventures. Such people are widely pursued. Their names appear on lists, and, as a result, they have their choice of a large number of promising projects. Generally speaking, they are a difficult mark for a young filmmaker without important credits.

There are also people who make a practice of investing a small percentage of their assets in highly speculative enterprises. These people are always worth talking to, and they may decide to go with you on a hunch or merely because they like your personal style.

Then there are amateurs, people who happen to like movies and are looking for a way to be connected with them. Of all the different types of outsiders, the amateurs may be the easiest to approach.

In approaching all prospective investors, you have to make a conscious analysis of the appeal of your material. If you are making a skin flick or a motorcycle story or something along those lines, then obviously you don't go to someone who thinks of himself as a patron of the arts. On the other hand, if you are doing something on race relations, or ecology, or that is avant-garde in style, you don't go to people who are looking to make a quick killing. By examining your project carefully and determining which type of investor it is likely to appeal to, you are in a position to concentrate your search.

Once you're inside the door, the result will depend on the impression you make. Great enthusiasm, self-confidence, and personal commitment are qualities to which people respond, more often than not on a subconscious level. Either they feel you've got it, or they feel you don't. They believe in your potential and reliability, or they are suspicious and think you are trying to put something over on them. No matter what you do, there will be people whom you will not be able to turn on. Beware of the type of person who will lead you along, either because he likes to play games, or because he is incapable of giving a direct answer (there are a surprising number of such people). The moment you sense this problem, you will save yourself a lot of time and disappointment by dropping them fast and going on to someone else.

(5) There is a myth that the best people to approach are "rich people." Naturally, prospective investors have to have money, but the idea that very wealthy people with huge inherited fortunes are amenable to investments in films is mostly mistaken. In the first place, very rich people aren't interested in making money. Secondly, their money is often tied up in trusts and they are surrounded by conservative financial advisors who are not apt to look kindly on an investment in a film. Thirdly, such people are extremely wary about being "taken." In short, it doesn't make much sense to pitch a project as a "quick killing" to a person who has $10,000,000. The only reason such a person might go with you is because he knows you and wants to help you out.

Sometimes you will hear that so-and-so gave $30,000 to a certain political campaign, or $50,000 to cancer research, or $100,000 to his alma mater. All this means is that the person has a lot of money, and that he is interested in politics, medical research, or education. People tend to confine their contributions to an area of personal interest. Because they have been generous in one area does not necessarily mean they will be generous in another.

(6) When you are looking for investors, you should be properly prepared with documentation. This means, first of all, that you should have worked out a

financial structure with the help of an attorney who specializes in theatrical law. This financial structure, whether it is a corporation or a limited partnership company or whatever, should be fully and clearly described in a carefully worded prospectus. The prospectus should explain exactly what an investor will get for his money: what his position will be in terms of recoupment, his percentage of possible profits, what other liabilities he may incur, what loans, liens, interest charges, percentages, and deferments will be owed or paid to or held by other people, and what you, the filmmaker, will receive as fees and as a percentage.

The prospectus should include a detailed budget for the production and biographical information about yourself and any other principals who may be involved. The prospective investor should be given a copy of the screenplay, and should have an opportunity to screen any other films you have made.

In preparing a prospectus, and also in any oral presentations you make, you should be very careful not to overstate the possibilities of earning profits, or even the chances of recoupment. There are many reasons for this, some of them legal, but the best reason is that everyone knows that an investment in an independent feature entails a high risk, and that total wipe-out is possible. To pretend otherwise may be to give the impression that you are a hustler, in the pejorative sense of the word.

You can expect some of the people you approach to question you very closely on the financial arrangements of the production company, and also about certain items in your budget. Usually they are probing, trying to determine if you really know what you're doing. The only way you can cope with such questions is to have a thorough grasp of the legal, financial, and budgetary aspects of your project.

(7) **When you go out to raise money, you must be realistic.** There is a point at which trying to raise money for a film becomes futile. This happens when unknown and inexperienced people try to put together a feature for $200,000 or $300,000. Unless they have a very significant prime investor, it is almost impossible. On the other hand, there is no question that anyone who is persistent enough and who cares enough and works hard enough can raise $50,000 or $60,000. It may take him a long time—it may take him more than a year—but it can be done, it is being done, and the only requirement is total devotion and a project that has merit.

Money-raising cannot be approached in a frivolous manner. You cannot expect to raise anything by going around to cocktail parties and asking everyone you meet for money. If you do this, people will at first be amused, and eventually will find you a bore.

There are many people promoting film projects and looking for private investors, and there are many investors who have been taken by phony and irresponsible filmmakers. One is in competition with the first group, and one suffers on account of the second. The better your screenplay, the sounder your financial structure, the more precise your budget preparation and the more extensive your personal credentials, the easier it will be to beat out the competition and avoid being connected with the phonies.

A warning: sometimes, late at night, after a great deal of drinking or a great deal of grass, a person may become very expansive, reach for his checkbook and write a check for a huge amount of money. The next morning, brimming with happiness, you will present his check at the bank only to discover that payment has already been stopped, there are insufficient funds, or the account is defunct. The lesson: just as there are many phonies hustling investors, so there are phony investors hustling filmmakers.

(8) **You should be willing and able to offer inducements.** This means that if someone helps you raise money, then that person is entitled to a percentage of your share of the profits. You should also not hesitate to offer screen credit—an associate producership, an executive producership, even a co-producership—to anyone who helps you raise a substantial amount. Screen credit costs you nothing to give, and it may mean a great deal to someone else. As for percentages of profits, you should be extremely eager to assign a large portion of these to someone who gets you the money to pay your production costs. Your main object, after all, is to make a successful film which will lead to professional financing the next time around; even if you give away most of your first picture, the payoff in terms of your future career makes such a renunciation academic.

(9) **The filmmaker must fulfill his obligations to his investors.** His first responsibility is to be honest with them at all times and to protect their investments from being wasted or stolen. Second, the filmmaker has a responsibility to complete the project in the form in which it was presented and at the cost at which it was budgeted. If he does these things, then, no matter what happens, even if the film does not sell, he has met his obligations and the investors can never say that they were "had."

The relationship between an artist and his patrons is always a difficult one. In most cases, all protestations to the contrary, the people who pay for the creation of a work of art want something for their money. Sometimes they want profits, sometimes they only want their money back; they may desire glory and excitement, or they may demand the never-ending gratitude of the artist. Some of these returns are very difficult to give, but investors are at least entitled to good treatment. When someone invests in a picture, he usually does so because he believes in the filmmaker. This is a very great compliment and it should be returned in some fashion. Certainly investors are entitled to frequent progress reports, frequent financial statements, a first look at the finished result, and as much of the fun and excitement of the filmmaking process as can be practically shared.

(10) **Money-raising is extremely difficult and there is no single proven approach to it.** Everyone who has been able to raise enough to make an independent feature has done so in a unique way. In most cases, the difference between success and failure has been determined by one or more strokes of luck. This has usually meant connecting with someone with a lot of money and establishing a great deal of instant rapport. One can go for six months without having any such luck, and then, suddenly, lightning strikes. In the end, there are two very important things to remember: you must never give up, and you must never be inhibited about asking anyone, no matter who he is, to help you out.

A final note: Young filmmakers often complain that they don't know people with money. If this is the case, then they should make a point of meeting such people. It may be as important to their professional life as learning how to operate a camera or stage a scene.   •

Rehearsing

If you want exceptional performances, then you must rehearse. This does not mean that it is sufficient to rehearse a scene on the set just before that scene is to be shot. On-the-set rehearsals have mechanical value, and they provide a means of refreshing a scene and warming up the performers. However, emotional concentration under these circumstances is extremely difficult, and the pressure of having thirty or so people standing around, receiving premium wages, while you do a few run-throughs is nearly unbearable.

It is a great indulgence to bring actors to a set, introduce them, and rehearse them to a point where they can play a scene above the level of television-series acting. Many professional actors pride themselves on being able to deliver a good performance under these conditions; in Hollywood, one tells an actor exactly what he is to do, and he does it. The result is competent, professional, and sufficient, but it is never brilliant, startling, or moving. The tendency always is to subordinate the emotional to the mechanical and to play along lines that skirt cliché. On the big screen, where perfection in the smallest parts can give a picture great quality and immeasurable richness, this kind of I'm-a-pro-and-I-can-do-anything-you-want-acting is not good enough.

The only way you can ever get brilliant performances is to work with your actors in long, concentrated rehearsal sessions. Scenes must be rehearsed and improvised and explored and built. There must be time to try different things, to define objectives, to examine and reexamine meanings and nuances. There must be an opportunity to revise dialogue and instill conviction. But above all, the greatest value of rehearsals is the opportunity they provide for the creation of familiarity, for collaborators to know and understand one another and to establish working relationships. The best work comes from people who are friends, and friendship can be built in rehearsals. For this reason, dinners, evenings together, bull sessions, and other forms of contact can be thought of as rehearsals.

If a filmmaker believes in intense rehearsals, not only with principal performers, but also with actors who will play minor roles, then he knows that he must make sacrifices in other areas. Beginning several weeks before the commencement of photography, he is going to have very little time available for making production decisions, giving final approval to locations, wardrobes, etc. If he throws himself into rehearsals, he is not going to be able to deal with many of these things, and he is going to have to delegate certain of his responsibilities to trustworthy associates. There are risks whenever a filmmaker does this, but in the final crisis-ridden weeks prior to shooting, he must set up priorities. The artistic payoff of intense rehearsals is so great that he may well decide to give them first attention.

Releases

Everyone knows the importance of obtaining releases, but on low-budget films people often get sloppy, and the consequences are occasionally disastrous. There are people who are always looking for ways to slap law suits on filmmakers, and when filmmakers fail to get releases (not only from extras, and from the parents of minors who appear in a film, but also for the use of locations), they are asking for trouble. There are several films with vast underground reputations which have never been distributed because someone forgot to get a release or made misrepresentations about what he was doing.

Nine out of ten people will sign a release without any trouble. When someone does balk, it is usually not worth your time trying to convince him. It saves a lot of hassles if you get the releases first, before you shoot, rather than discovering too late that a troublemaker is going to force you to shoot the scene again. When you are shooting candid material, the issue becomes more vague. You should be careful about exploiting people in the frame who might later claim you have held them up to public ridicule.

Music licenses are also terribly important. Everyone knows that one has to pay for the rights to any music that is laid into the sound track of a picture, but people occasionally forget that if a radio is on when you're shooting, and someone like Bob Dylan just happens to be singing and his song is interwoven with your dialogue, then you are either going to have to shoot the scene again, pay a fortune, or face some very heavy claims later on.

Ruthlessness

Perhaps the saddest comment one can make about the situation of the would-be filmmaker in America is that he must learn to be ruthless.

It is a cruel paradox that those qualities of sensitivity and humanity and integrity that are so necessary to the artistic success of a film may never be exercised unless the filmmaker also has the ability to be ruthless. To put it another way, some who are most likely to succeed as filmmakers may well be those who are least qualified artistically. The pushiest, most ruthless, most arrogant and insensitive director may find himself at the top, while the most sensitive, honest, and humane director may never make a feature film. This has always been the dilemma of the American filmmaker, and it is still the case.

Nobody wants to hear this (and nobody really wants to say it), but it's unrealistic not to recognize and face the truth, which is that success and survival in the world of film cannot be achieved by talent alone—that in a world where dog-eat-dog is the operating principle, and money and power are the levers of control, ruthlessness is a quality that must be cultivated as much as talent and vision.

The reasons are pretty obvious. One, of course, is the way the film business is structured and the nature of the men who control it. Filmmaking, at times, comes down to simple ego warfare. The man or woman with an artistic vision is particularly vulnerable to the brutality and ignorance of the businessman, and an ability to fight, an instinctive resistance to giving up, can make the difference between winning and losing these endless battles.

The great expense of feature filmmaking sets it apart from the other arts. The painter only needs his talent and a few dollars worth of paint to do his work. For the writer, the poet, and the composer, it is the same. But the filmmaker needs a great deal of money, and to get that money he must become a salesman—a salesman of himself as an artistically talented and financially responsible individual with a project that is commercially viable. No major company will back a film which its executives do not think will make money. The fact that they are often mistaken is beside the point. They simply are not patrons of the arts. A few publishers will publish a book when they believe it has merit, even if they think it has little commercial appeal. In such cases they are prepared to take a loss. No film company has ever or will ever indulge a filmmaker in this way.

Competition is another reason that ruthlessness is so important. The world is filled with men and women who want to make feature films, and very few of them will succeed. The others are jealous and frustrated and knocking at the door. At every turn there are people who want someone else to fail so their chances will improve. Directors, including some of those considered most pure, revel in the bad reviews of their peers. It's a terrible thing, but there is just not enough money to go around.

Every day film people employ unethical business practices which are unthinkable in other industries. This may account for the fact that nearly everyone in the film business is constantly involved in litigation. Suits and counter-suits are common occurrences. Contracts are broken, commitments are ignored, money disappears, and double-dealing is rampant. Just because major companies are listed on the stock exchange is no reason to expect anything but the most ruthless and primitive behavior by their managements. There are, of course, exceptions. There are people who do keep their word, who do act in good faith, and for whom Machiavelli's *The Prince* is not regular bed-side reading. But those who follow the Golden Rule are very few.

A filmmaker confronting this situation has two choices. He can go in and fight and try to change the system—and if he succeeds, everyone else will owe him an enormous debt. The second choice is to learn to play the game. Whichever choice he makes, he will have to be ruthless.

If the would-be filmmaker remains pure and pristine, he can look forward to many delightful evenings sitting around with his friends talking about that low-budget film he's *not* going to make. The more he complains about the system and curses the establishment and indulges in hurt feelings and refuses to step down into the gutter where the in-fighting takes place, the less his chances of making his films. If he is content to talk about an imaginary film, all right. But if he really wants to see his fantasy on the big screen, then he must be prepared to go out and fight for it.

It is so incredibly difficult to launch an independent feature—to raise the money and organize the production and bring it in on budget and do the completion work and sell the final result to a distributor—that sometimes the artistic problems, which should occupy a filmmaker's attention, begin to take second place. He must not let this happen. The filmmaker must be an artist and a businessman at the same time. He cannot afford to be weak in either area, for only if he is strong in both is there a chance (although no guarantee) that he will succeed.

This is not to imply that he has to become a beast or make a Faustian pact with the devil. It does mean that when he must choose between being a good human being and making his film, he will choose the film. For the filmmaker there is no choice, and it is the tragedy of his profession that such choices are constantly presenting themselves for decision. If he has to fire a friend because the friend is messing up his picture, he will fire him. He will suffer for it and remorse of this kind may make him bitter—make him question whether or not he really wants to make films. If it is any consolation (and it probably isn't), he should know that every filmmaker has these moments of self-questioning. The inevitability of having to wield power in a ruthless manner may be one of the principal reasons that filmmakers burn themselves out so fast.

No matter how talented he is and how powerful he becomes, sooner or later the filmmaker is going to get screwed by the philistines. Fred Zinnemann was about to shoot his version of one of the greatest novels of this century, Malraux' *Man's Fate,* after nearly three years of full-time preproduction work, when new management at M-G-M cancelled the project. The same thing happened to Stanley Kubrick and his *Napoleon.* It has happened to Sam Packinpah and Richard Lester and countless others. If it can happen to artists like these, think of what can happen to a filmmaker when he's starting off and is vulnerable.

Frankly, there is no way to deal with the philistines except on their own terms. If they employ jungle tactics, then the filmmaker must employ them too, in self-defense. If ruthlessness come naturally to him, then he is ahead of the game. If it doesn't, he will have to find some school where he can take a course in ruthlessness. The best school may be the firing line of the independent feature. If he starts out to make one, and it reaches the screen, he is ruthless.

Screen Ratios

The screen ratio, or aspect ratio, as it is sometimes called—the ratio of the height to the width of the screen image—is a much talked about but ultimately hopeless subject. If you decide to shoot in CinemaScope or some other ultrawide process, you are reasonably safe, but if you choose one of the normal ratios, 1.33, 1.66, or 1.85, you are going to end up unhappy, and there is nothing you can do about it.

Theatre owners and projectionists just don't care. No matter how precise the instructions you attach to the leaders of the film, and no matter how many times you underline the preferred ratio on the carrying cases, your film will be projected whatever way strikes their fancy, or causes them the least amount of work. There are first-run theatres in New York where they project films at weird ratios no one has ever heard of, just because that's the way the theatre was designed and nobody cares enough to have it changed.

The most common ratio is 1.85, and so despite the fact that many filmmakers find this a difficult ratio—one that is not particularly amenable to good composition—they use it anyway, thinking that it's the way their film is most likely to be projected. Others choose

1.66, the famous "golden rectangle" of Renaissance painters, knowing but not caring that 90 percent of the time their film will not be projected the way the images were composed. As for 1.33, there is an idea held by people who should know better that this is the ratio of amateurs, and that modified wide-screen ratios are better.

In the end, the filmmaker should shoot his film the way he wants, making certain that microphones are completely out of the 1.33 frame, and that titles and important action are within the 1.85 cutoff. When his picture receives its world premiere, he can go to the theatre, plead his case, and throw himself on the mercy of the barbarians.

Screenings and Screening Rooms

There seems to be a conspiracy among projectionists to savage filmmakers at important screenings. If they don't miss the changeover cues, then you can be sure they will break the film, the sound will go bad, or the first roll will come on upside-down.

Like post office clerks and those who issue drivers' licenses, projectionists love to exert their power and torture the public. Their unions operate on a seniority system, with the oldest and most bored projectionists taking the plushest jobs at first-run theatres. The fact that one can pay $3.00 to see a picture and then suffer because a projector is out-of-focus is a great and continuing scandal in the industry.

There is very little you can do about bad projection. Sometimes it helps to go into the booth before a screening and try to make friends with the projectionist. Compliment him on the equipment, speak with wonder of the brilliance and dexterity it must take to make reel changes so accurately, and tell him you've decided to screen with him because you've heard he's the best in the business. One out of ten times he will put himself out and give you a respectable show.

When choosing a screening room, think carefully about your audience. There are times when a really funky screening room can have great mystique. For instance, for a screening for wealthy investors it makes a lot of sense to choose a room in a remote neighborhood. This gives the occasion a sense of adventure. For poverty-stricken actors and sweaty crew members, you can use reverse psychology, booking the poshest room in town.

One hostile viewer spewing forth bad "vibes" can ruin a screening. Beware of people who talk out loud during lyrical sequences, or sit in the front row and whisper. In a screening there are all sorts of subconscious factors at work: the loudness or softness of the track; the extent to which the room is filled; the depth of the silence. Even when you show the same film in the same room to a different audience, you can sense, without looking at their faces, that one screening is going better than another.

As a general rule, if your film has lots of laughs, it's better to fill the room up and bring in some ringers to guffaw at prearranged moments. If the film is serious, it's sometimes effective to show it to only a few people at a time, thereby engendering the respectfulness that people reserve for a serious work of art.

If you want to make some introductory remarks to

an audience before a screening, be careful. The worst thing you can do is to explain a film before you've shown it. Nothing turns people off so much as a director who insists on getting up first and begging for their sympathy. If you must speak, confine yourself to some comments on the color correction, or something technical like that.

You can make a prospective distributor feel very important by giving him a "Darryl Zanuck Complex." This is achieved by holding the screening without anyone else in the room. The "Darryl Zanuck Complex" puts the distributor into a receptive mood by appealing to his fantasies of power.

When showing a film to a group of square middle-aged distributors, it sometimes helps to sprinkle in some hippie types who will exclaim "groovy, man!" and slap your hand after the show. Even if the distributors are not too fond of your picture, this kind of exhibition can change their minds because they are obsessed with what "the kids will think."

Screenplays, Treatments, Outlines, Properties and Concepts

SCREENPLAYS

(1) A certain sign that a screenplay has been written by a hack is the inclusion of a large number of instructions to the director and the editor, such as: "Cut to

a new angle"; "Freeze-frame and dissolve"; and "She walks toward the door, stops, looks at him, and sits down as the camera dollies into a closeup of her hands." Writers who insist upon directing on paper befuddle their readers, bore their directors, and usually end up demonstrating their ignorance of screen technique.

The best screenwriters devote their efforts to telling a story by inventing scenes, structuring them into sequences, and writing dialogue that creates characters and delineates their relationships. Anything else is wasted effort and is usually inserted to fatten a script and to give the impression that the writer has mastery over something he likes to call his "craft." When you pick up a screenplay and find that the first two words are "Fade in" and then have to read a long and ingenious description of how the credit titles will be displayed, you know you are in for a long afternoon.

(2) The screenwriter must convey to his readers not only the substance of his scenes, but also their mood and their meaning. He can achieve this more readily by an intelligent, judicious, and even poetic use of the English language than by employing technical jargon. For example, it is possible to write in a description of the location of a certain scene that "you can smell the gun oil in the room." Everybody knows that odors cannot be conveyed by the screen, but the sense of the room may be better explained by the phrase "you can smell the gun oil" than by a long architectural description and a lengthy list of props. On the other hand, there are certain literary leaps which look very good on paper but are less helpful when it comes time to shoot. The phrase "the sky is like a bruise" sounds very nice, but one wonders exactly how the scene can

be shot without waiting around for weeks for the sky to achieve that particular color and configuration.

(3) People say that writing style has no meaning in a screenplay except in the dialogue portions. Style doesn't matter, the argument goes, because the only style that is important to a film is that which is imparted by the director. This would be true if screenplays were merely written accounts of how a film is to look, who the characters are, what they say, and how the story unravels. Unfortunately this is not always the case. A good and workable account of a proposed film can be extremely dull reading, and this can make its financing difficult. A screenplay, therefore, in addition to its obvious purposes, must be good reading for people who make decisions about financing projects and who usually hate to read. In other words, a screenplay should be a presentation that sells itself.

(4) In the theatre, the actors, the director, and everyone else work for the writer. Their job is to make the play come alive; to find the best way of serving the playwright's conception. In film, where the director is the central creator, everyone, including the writer, works for him. In good collaborative relationships, the screenwriter and the director share a concept, and it is then the writer's job to put that concept into words so that, at a later time, the director can put it into images. The director needs a screenplay in order to present a project, and also as a working document for himself, his actors, his cameraman, his art director, his production manager, and all the other people who will contribute to the production. Because a screenplay is a working document and not a final result, it is not a work of art, as is, for example, a play or a musical composition. A screenplay is much closer to a

blueprint. There is no denying that the screenwriter is an essential collaborator, and that his work is the first creative act in the making of a film, but his place is necessarily subordinate to that of the filmmaker, and if this state of affairs does not satisfy him, then he is better off writing in some other form.

TREATMENTS

(1) A treatment, as opposed to a screenplay, is not a document that can be used to make a film; it is a document that is required for artificial reasons. A treatment—a straightforward prose account of a film —may be requested because a producer needs a short and highly readable presentation of a project for busy and/or illiterate executives so he can show how a property he has bought is being altered, adapted, and, in fact, "treated" for transfer to the screen; or as a point of departure for discussions which he has the nerve to call "story-conferences." The real reason a writer is asked to prepare a treatment, however, is because this short and irrelevant form is the quickest and cheapest way to pick his brains and extract his ideas.

(2) A treatment can have value to a screenwriter as a sort of sketch of how he is going to adapt a property. In this sense, it can be considered a memorandum from a screenwriter to himself and his filmmaker collaborator. Unfortunately the kind of notes a screenwriter would prepare for himself and the format that is desired by a producer are two very different things.

(3) If a treatment were written for a film like *La Strada*—a film, in other words, that is more dependent

upon style than upon story—it would look ridiculous. A treatment of *La Strada* would be rejected by every producing organization in America. This may indicate the limitation of treatments: films that are not heavily plotted, and which are not particularly linear in design, are not amenable to presentation in this form.

OUTLINES

Producers often request an outline, and then, if they like the outline, a treatment, and then, if they like the treatment, a screenplay, and then a revised screenplay, etc. Thus an outline, like a treatment, becomes an inexpensive preliminary phase of a screenwriting contract. Actually, the only value of an outline is as an internal document for use by a writer and a filmmaker. Producers and studio executives like outlines because they are very short and can be read in five minutes. Another reason they like them is because it makes them very nervous to pay people to sit around and talk; they feel better if they are paying for a thing, even if it's only three or four pages of writing.

PROPERTIES

Nearly every motion picture made in the United States is based upon or adapted from a novel, a play, a short story, a biography, a work of nonfiction, a popular song, or some other work in some other medium. These primal works are called "properties," which connotes exactly the way they are perceived. The dependence of American filmmakers upon properties is very depressing, and unless it is changed, unless the best writers begin to create directly for the screen, there will continue to be a shortage of first-class films.

The traditional dependence upon properties has turned filmmaking into a parasitic profession. The difficulty for many directors is that they have become so accustomed to the convention of adaptation that they act as if they have nothing to say of their own. They flounder about, reading galley proofs, bidding on books, paying out enormous sums, all the time desperately looking for stories to retell. They go through life transferring stories from one medium to another, expressing themselves solely through style, forgetting the pleasure that comes from creating synthetically, inventing substance as well as form. It is the job of the filmmaker, as opposed to the director who is for hire, to create material for the screen. He may collaborate with a writer because he can't write good dialogue, but he has his own ideas, his own conceptions, and does not have to wait around until someone else thinks up something that appeals to his taste.

8½ and *Hiroshima Mon Amour* are very exciting works because they were originally conceived as films. *The Arrangement* was disappointing because even though it was written by a filmmaker of the first rank, it was conceived as a novel, and when it appeared on the screen it had lost whatever merits it may have had in its original form.

The problem, of course, is that the best writers don't want to work in a secondary role. One solution is for writers to become filmmakers, to write with images as well as with words. This leads to an interesting speculation: it may be that the greatest screen artists will be men who in another age would have written books.

CONCEPTS

The creation of the concept is the most important act in the preparation of a film. A film without a concept is more apt to look like something cooked up in ten days at Universal Studios for a television premiere than something suitable for the big screen.

A concept is a statement of intention: what a story is about and how it is going to be expressed. It is, in part, a determination whether a film will be realistic or surrealistic, satiric or straight, funny or sad, warm or cool, austere or opulent. Everything—the dialogue, performances, photography, directorial style, art direction, editing, even the advertising and promotion— should derive from the concept. The concept concerns the look of a film, how it will be played, and how it will affect the audience. Without a concept, a film is likely to be a mess: either too bland, too boring, or too disjointed; without style, without impact, without a sense of itself.

Interestingly, executives at studios are not very concerned about concepts. They want to know about the plot, the stars, and what the film is going to cost. They think, quite rightly, that the development and implementation of the concept is the director's job; that they are paying him to worry about that. They fail to understand, however, that if they do not know what he has in mind, they are in a very poor position to judge the commercial viability of his project.

A concept is often very simple, and can be expressed in a few lines:

"I'm going to make a film that will lacerate the new Hollywood. I'm going to satirize the hell out of the hip, young, successful, beautiful people in their tie-dyes and buckskin. I'm going to expose their useless, decadent life-style in a series of merciless vignettes."

"I want to tell the story of Jesus Christ in the simplest possible way. I'm not going to present it as a fable or as a world-shattering event; I'm going to take a documentary approach and come up with something unpretentious and gritty. When Christ, in my film, says, 'I am the son of God,' he is going to use the tone of voice of a simple carpenter saying 'good morning.' "

"I'm going to make a horror film that will make the audience scream. There will be surprises, twists and turns in the plot, and also changing points of view. The audience is going to be drawn into a fantastical world of paranoia and terror."

These very brief concepts may tell a lot more about a film than some long description of the story, the characters, and the plot. Of course, a concept is not always so easily expressed. Sometimes, when a concept is sophisticated, it is very difficult to put it into succinct language. But it doesn't really matter if a concept is ever written down or even stated directly; the important thing is that it exist, that it be shared by the writer and the filmmaker, and that it be implemented in every phase from screenplay to answer print.

Selling Out

There is a great deal of miscomprehension about the expression "selling out" and what it means in reference to film. From time to time you will hear someone say that a certain filmmaker has "sold out." When asked for details and a clear definition of the phrase, the speaker will explain that the man in question "took a lot of money and went to Hollywood."

Such a judgment usually reflects less upon the character of the accused than upon that of the accuser. To reproach another person for selling out is a very common habit of those who are filled with envy and looking for a way to rationalize their own position as a "loser."

Back in the 1950s, a girl who went to bed with many different men was called a whore. Actually a whore is someone who sleeps with men for money, whether she likes them or not, which is quite different from actively sleeping around for pleasure. Similarly, a filmmaker who goes to Hollywood and earns a great deal of money does not necessarily prostitute himself. He sells out only when he performs work that he despises in order to obtain something other than artistic satisfaction.

The great myth—that selling out is being famous, making money, and creating films that are successful at the box office—is accepted by young filmmakers as a defense against the hurts and anguish of their own struggles. Actually, selling out is to betray oneself, and nothing more.

If a filmmaker wants to make Doris Day pictures, and if he is talented at making Doris Day pictures, then his Doris Day pictures do not signify he is a sellout or a hack. To push the point even further, when a filmmaker whose *metier* is Doris Day pictures fakes an avant-garde film so that he can be screened at the Museum of Modern Art and obtain the approbation of that particular establishment, he is selling out his talent as much as the avant-garde filmmaker who tires of his garret, goes to Hollywood, and tries to direct Doris Day.

An amusing and frequent experience in Hollywood is to spend an evening with a filmmaker who whines and writhes and exhibits self-disgust because, he tells you, he has sold out his talent for worldly goods. Most of the time such people are working at the height of their powers, and their claim that they have sold out is a means to convince themselves that their potential is greater than their work. They are no less pathetic than the filmmaker who tells you that if he were not so independent and incorruptible, he could have amassed a fortune instead of starving for his art.

In the end people do what they want to do, and most of the time they find a proper niche. Probably fewer than one filmmaker in a hundred is so pure that he would not hire himself out if he thought that doing so would lead to a chance to work for himself.

Just as financial success and public recognition are not cachets of quality, so poverty and failure are not proofs of artistic integrity. The filmmaker who is quick to accuse a co-worker of selling out, being a hack, and other heinous crimes, might do well to examine the dimensions of his own talent. He might decide that he is selling *himself* too short.

Sex and the Filmmaker

(1) Sexism is prevalent in the film industry. The only area where women have achieved equal status is in the profession of acting, and that is because there they are a necessity. Women have been reasonably

successful as agents and screenwriters. There have been some prominent women film editors, casting directors, and story editors. Very few women are in the upper echelons of film-producing organizations, and hardly any are directors, producers, or directors of photography. In speaking of women filmmakers, only two names come readily to mind: Agnes Varda and Shirley Clarke.

(2) At the same time that the filmmaker became a superstar, he also became a sex object. This is not to say that there are hordes of groupies surrounding his home, but that he is frequently pursued by women for no other reason than that he is a culture hero and is believed to wield power. However, since the filmmaker is not a performing artist, there are no advantages he can gain from this kind of attention, aside from the obvious one of having a full and various sex life.

(3) When a filmmaker has sexual relations with a member of his cast, he takes certain risks. He gives one person an opportunity to wield power in a "special relationship," which that person is very likely to abuse, and which will cause deep and justifiable resentment among other cast members. Common sense should inform him that these risks are not worth taking.

(4) It is common for actors and actresses within a film company to have love affairs with each other. This happens with special frequency when the company is on location. Sometimes these relationships contribute to the work, sometimes they have no effect on it, and sometimes they have a disastrous effect. An astute filmmaker knows about all the sexual activities of members of his company, and tries to use this knowledge to advantage.

(5) Jokes about couch-casting and actresses who obtain parts by sleeping with directors and producers are probably truer than most people think.

(6) When you ask an actor and an actress to perform a love scene, it is a requirement that they rehearse by engaging in a good deal of preliminary making-out. An exception may be made if the scene deals with their first sexual encounter.

(7) It is distracting when a script-girl insists on working in a bikini among an all-male crew.

(8) For years sex scenes were shot in one of two ways: either as highly stylized and overly lyrical encounters, or as sweaty and gritty acts. French directors were traditionally the best at staging sex: they employed good taste and created an illusion of eroticism. American directors were traditionally the worst: they were overly fond of visual metaphors such as displays of fire works, feet crushing flowers or cutting to the barn for a symphony of stallions' hoofbeats and mares' whinnies.

(9) The scene in *Five Easy Pieces* in which Karen Black has a cataclysmic orgasm, and the scene in *Ryan's Daughter* in which Sarah Miles has several restrained and extremely elegant orgasms, are breakthroughs in the art of filming sex.

(10) Some performers relate to the motion-picture camera as if it were a sex object; in effect, they make love to the camera. (Some very fine actors do not have "camera awareness" and this may account for the fact that many good actors are not stars.) The camera-as-sex-object is a most interesting phenomenon. When a filmmaker discovers that one of his performers is turned on by the camera, he is in a position to achieve remarkable results.

Shooting Ratios

(1) The shooting ratio—the ratio between the amount of footage shot and the amount finally used in a film—is a subject of great fascination to film students. One of the first questions they ask in a session with a filmmaker is, "What was your shooting ratio?" as if this has anything to do with the achievement of excellence. A lot of directors respond with a blank stare because they really don't know what their ratio was.

(2) Shooting ratios can be very important on certain types of films, and of little consequence on others. On a major production, when someone goes out to shoot for a hundred or more days, he doesn't concern himself with the shooting ratio. Raw stock, in such cases, is like cigarettes, and the filmmaker becomes a chain smoker.

On a low-budget film, though, where the filmmaker has limited funds and is fighting against the inexperience of actors and crew and coping with the problems of sound and light that occur on location, then the shooting ratio might well affect the final result.

(3) The shooting ratio is often dictated by the style of a film. If a picture is shot in long, designed shots with actors who are well rehearsed, then it becomes feasible, as in the case of *Greetings!*, to shoot at a ratio of less than 5 to 1. If the picture is made in a more academic style—shooting a number of different angles of each scene—then anything between 10 and 20 to 1 is realistic. If a filmmaker attempts to improvise a

film before three cameras running all the time, the shooting ratio can easily exceed 80 to 1.

(4) The shooting ratio depends not only on the number of angles, but also on the number of takes. There are directors who make a practice of shooting many takes, sometimes as many as twenty on every shot. People who study the rushes of such directors usually conclude that there is no improvement between take four and take twenty; in fact, after a certain number of takes, not only is there a point of diminishing returns, but also a point at which the acting begins to get worse. When a director makes a practice of shooting twenty takes of every shot, there may be good reason to believe that he is insecure, on an immensely neurotic ego trip, or else is out to break a performer.

(5) On a low-budget production, when a scene isn't working, it's not very intelligent to keep shooting film in the hope that a miracle will occur and the scene will suddenly improve. After a certain point, the filmmaker must ask himself whether there is not something wrong in the conception or weak in the performers that no amount of shooting will overcome. In such cases, he may be wise to rewrite the scene, or stage it in an entirely different way.

(6) There are directors who commonly ask for another take after a good take has been achieved because, they say, they need it for "safety." If this means that another take is a precaution against a technical malfunction, then one wonders why the protection shot is going to be exposed on the same roll as the shot that is being protected.

(7) There are directors who specialize in action films and who attribute their success, in interviews with

eager film buffs, to the great variety of angles which they shoot. Such directors end up servicing their editors, on the theory that if one supplies enough footage, something good can be made from it. This approach cannot be used on a low-budget film, and, in any case, it is a method employed by hacks.

(8) When a filmmaker is working on location, certain occurrences can increase the shooting ratio. Airplanes interfere with the dialogue track, trucks backfire in the middle of intimate scenes, and the weather can be in a state of constant flux. (One thinks of those miserable days in which clouds move fast and one is caught, from moment to moment, between brilliant sunlight and an overcast sky.)

Dubbing is one way out of wasting a lot of time and film, and the filmmaker must weigh its disadvantages against the tightness of his shooting schedule and the limitations of his shooting ratio. As for bad weather, there is nothing that can be done about it. The intelligent solution is to go to a cover location; it is stupid to burn up film while hoping for a meteorological miracle.

(9) It is difficult to control the shooting ratio of a cinéma vérité film unless one knows exactly what one is trying to do. For example, if a filmmaker is shooting a picture in which he simply follows a person around, hoping and waiting for something interesting to happen, he can shoot miles of film to no apparent end. But if a man is under sentence of death, and the sentence is due to be carried out in three days, then the filmmaker knows that he has only to shoot for three days and in the end the man will die or be reprieved.

The same goes for shooting a rock concert. The filmmaker knows that a certain number of people are going to sing a certain number of songs in a certain span of time, and when he decides to cover the concert with a certain number of cameras running a certain number of hours, he can predict the shooting ratio and properly budget the film. However, if he follows a rock group around waiting for a story to unfold, he can get lucky in a week or shoot for six months to no avail. It's like the gambler who doubles his bet after every loss; unless he has infinite capital, the doubling system cannot work.

16 and 35

There are only two reasons to shoot an independent feature in 16mm. The first is camera mobility and the second is money.

If the feature is a cinéma vérité documentary like *Gimme Shelter*, it must be shot in 16mm. Even if the film is scripted, if it requires a great deal of sync-sound hand-held camera work, 16mm. may be the only solution, at least for those portions that are shot hand-held. (It is not impossible to shoot hand-held in 35mm., but very few cameramen can manage it well.)

The question of money is a little more complicated, and has to do almost totally with the shooting ratio. Roughly speaking and using approximate figures, the relative costs of shooting a ninety-minute feature at a ratio of 4 to 1, including the costs of blowing up, is just about the same in 16 and 35 color. If the film is to be shot at a ratio of 12 to 1 (which is realistic for a dramatic feature), then the cost of shooting in 35 is almost double the cost of shooting in 16. If the film is a cinéma vérité documentary with a shooting ratio of 40 to 1, then 16 will cost about a quarter of 35. It is immediately clear that the more one shoots, the greater the savings if 16 is used: the cost differential expands as the shooting ratio increases. If the film-maker can compute his shooting ratio in advance, he is in a position to properly analyze whether the savings of working in 16 are worth the decline in image quality.

There are a number of fine films that have reached the big screen blown up from 16mm. *Gimme Shelter*, *Goin' Down the Road*, *Don't Look Back*, *Salesman*, *Woodstock*, and *Monterey Pop* are particularly well known. But one film of extraordinary power, John Cassavetes' masterpiece *Faces*, breaks all the rules and makes a very important point.

Faces was shot in 16 black and white, and it has an extremely grainy appearance. There is little or no hand-held camera work, the shooting is more or less conventional, and the lighting verges on Hollywood-bad. Cassavetes shot in 16 to save money (he paid for the film himself and worked on it between other jobs). *Faces* is such an instructive example because it proves that when a film is really good, when the subject matter is strong and the acting is magnificent, then nobody cares whether it is grainy or in black and white or whatever. Audiences become so involved with the characters that all those things they expect to see in a movie theatre—rich color, lavish production values, orchestrated music, clear sound—cease to matter. In fact, it's probably true that the crude look of *Faces* contributes to its powerful effect—there are no lush distractions from the cruelty of its images.

No one wants his film to look bad, or to be grainy, or be soft, but *Faces* proves something very important that can be stated as an axiom: *If you have a choice between shooting a film that will not look particularly good in 16mm. and not shooting it at all, you really have no choice: you must always make the film, no matter the gauge, no matter the technical inferiority.* This may seem self-evident, but there are a lot of people who are still waiting around for a couple of hundred thousand dollars to fall into their hands because they think there's something cheap and amateurish about working in 16. They may be waiting around all their lives.

Stealing

The amount of stealing that takes place in the film industry is one of the most depressing phenomena of the filmmaker's life. Everyone, it seems, steals from everyone else.

(1) The most pernicious stealing takes place along a chain of people, each of whom, at one point, has his hands on the dollars that are paid at the box office: theatre employees steal from exhibitors, who steal from distributors, who steal from producers, who, in turn, steal from those participating in the income of a film. The filmmaker, who may own a percentage of the producer's profits, is at the end of this long chain of thieves whose livelihoods are totally dependent upon his vision and talent.

(2) People on production crews always steal little things: rolls of gaffer tape to repair the torn seats of their Volkswagens, a few choice props to decorate

their apartments, etc. Some are even so petty as to charge for a taxi when they have used a bus, or to gas up on "regular" and charge for "supreme." This kind of small-scale larceny can be tolerated, but when raw stock and equipment begin to disappear, toleration must stop.

(3) On every production there are things that get "lost." An examination of a list of "lost" items reveals something very interesting: there are no "lost" century stands, barn doors, and triangles, but there are a lot of "lost" exposure meters, lenses, and microphones. These items are "lost" all right—lost by reason of theft.

(4) It is interesting that whenever a set is struck, all sorts of strange trucks suddenly appear and begin to haul away lumber and hardware at an amazing speed.

(5) If there is one thing that is worse than a crooked cop, it is a crooked production manager. When the production manager, who is supposed to protect a film company against thieves, turns out to be a thief himself, it is a real problem, for he is in an excellent position to steal large amounts of material and cash, and he can bankrupt a low-budget production before shooting is halfway finished.

(6) Perhaps the reason that stealing is so rampant is that there exists a psychology, created in the heyday of Hollywood, that movies are one big rip-off. Film is seen as a business in which hucksters fleece rubes, in which entertainment that has no value is sold to people through hype. The result is a feeling that if the proverbial "they" (meaning, one supposes, the studios) are going to steal from the public, then each and every person connected with a film is entitled to his piece of the action too.

Talent and Balance

A filmmaker can learn to achieve fair results if he works hard and studies his craft, but if he is to rise above mediocrity, he must possess talent and balance. Neither can be studied, taught, or gained through experience.

Talent is natural ability, granted to only a few. Filmmaking has not produced many prodigies, perhaps because of its technical nature. Most filmmakers start off working in an awkward fashion, but if they have talent, it begins to show as soon as they achieve mastery of craft.

Balance—an instinct for what is right—is a more elusive gift. As the filter that refines raw talent and censors the excesses of genius, it is essential to greatness in all the arts.

Talent and balance are rarely apportioned equally, even among filmmakers of the first rank, but when they come together in a single filmmaker, as they do in Jean Renoir, then we tremble before the power of the screen.

It is sad to see a person struggling to become a filmmaker whom one knows does not have the talent to justify his suffering. One may find it an admirable trait of character in a person with modest talent and passable taste when he loves a form so much that he works to the limits of his abilities; however, we are interested in what is on the screen, and a well-made fantasy of a mediocre filmmaker who is functioning at his peak is a lot less interesting than the flawed fantasy of a genius.

People who want to be filmmakers must ask themselves a hard question. There is no point in going into something as difficult and painful as filmmaking unless one is confident that one has sufficient natural abilities to become one of the best. At the crux of the identity crisis of the would-be filmmaker is the question: "Have I the gifts to write with greatness upon the screen?" If he believes that he has, then he should not hesitate to join the fight. On the other hand, he should know that talent and balance cannot be faked because their presence or lack will show in every frame.

Television

There is much that can be said about television: its implications for a young director looking for a place to start out; the styleless style of TV series; the endless limitations of the little screen. There is one fact, however, that just about says it all: there is not a person who works in the creative end of dramatic television who does not wish he were making, writing, or performing in feature films.

Titles

(1) One of the surest signs that a picture is going to be bad is when the titles are made out of elaborate

optical effects, expensive and tricky animation, symbolic images, lettering that disintegrates and then recomposes, and other elements that West Coast producers like to characterize as "class."

(2) It is said that good titles set up a picture, conveying its mood and style to the audience. This is like saying that the way to grasp the spirit of a painting is to begin by looking at the signature. For years people have struggled to invent ingenious and unobtrusive ways of working credit titles into opening sequences, when the problem is so easily solved by simply putting titles at the beginning or the end of a film. There is a theory that an audience won't stand for a series of mood-setting opening shots unless titles are superimposed upon them. In truth, the public is always ready for a breakdown of artificial conventions, witness the acceptance of the dropping of "The End," once considered obligatory on the final frame.

(3) Most companies that specialize in title design perform a disservice to producers. Usually they deal in flash, which can give a false impression of a picture and can lead to audience letdown. How many times have we seen films with lively titles which died when the first scene was low-key?

(4) It is always amusing when the time comes in the cutting room to decide where the titles will go. People who haven't been seen in months suddenly reappear, the room crackles with tension and distrust, and there is a lot of astute listening to music in attempts to find the "zings"—bursts of music which subliminally cue the audience to the importance of the names.

(5) For years the chiefs of technical departments at Hollywood studios took screen credit for work actually

performed by their subordinates. This was a prerogative of their rank and gave them opportunities to acquire Academy Awards.

(6) Occasionally one sees a modest low-budget film with pretentious and expensive main titles. There is nothing more ludicrous than a filmmaker with limited funds wasting his money on titles when he should be putting every cent into shooting time and raw stock.

(7) It's a perfectly fair and, as a matter of fact, an amusing game to try to get one's name on the screen as many times as one can, but the ego trip becomes a little too transparent when a ten-minute student production exhibits the name of its creator more than three times.

(8) The phrase "a film by——" beneath the main title of a picture is a literal translation of "un film de——," a proper means of expressing auteurship in French, but a little forced in English. Unfortunately we do not yet have a foolproof and unpretentious means of expressing the credit due to a filmmaker, as opposed to that which is due a director-for-hire. Everything possible has been tried, and we only await the day when a filmmaker cuts his signature into the emulsion of his original negative in emulation of the great megalomaniac, Ettore Bugatti, who is reputed to have signed the hot engine blocks of his cars.

(9) There are people who believe that they have finally arrived when they see their names above the main title of a film. This space is usually reserved for movie stars and producer-directors of great bankability. The low-budget filmmaker can obtain this much coveted position by a single stroke of desire, and thus pave the way for his eventual recognition as a "heavy."

(10) Seeing one's name in a prominent position on the motion-picture screen has value, to many people, far beyond crass and despised money. The low-budget filmmaker must know how to present credits, which are of immeasurable value to people seeking fame, in exchange for services, without betraying the fact that they are the easiest and cheapest things he has to give.

(11) In contractual clauses that deal with credit titles, several things are important: the size and position of credits on positive prints of a film, and whether or not the particular credits must also be included in advertising and promotion. This latter point leads to the great hokeyness of film ads that are choked with names, including the inevitable and meaningless credit given to the laboratory that made the prints.

(12) The guilds that represent the interests of writers, directors, and actors have complex arbitration procedures for dealing with disputes over credit titles. What they seem unable to solve are problems that arise when an artist, particularly a director, wishes to have his name removed from a film because he feels that his work has been destroyed by the editing or additions of somebody else. The fact that one frequently reads about a filmmaker suing a production company over this very issue would seem to belie the claims of the studios that they recognize the filmmaker as the central artist of the cinema. They are content to massacre his footage and bad-mouth him in the industry, but they seem unwilling to allow him the right to remove his name from pictures that do not represent his work.

Turkeys

There are many kinds of turkeys. First is the film that opens to bad notices and an empty house and in which the losses—personal, artistic, and financial—are total. There are many examples of the "cold turkey"; one that comes to mind is *Cover Me Babe*.

Another kind of turkey is the film that goes "gobble-gobble" after it has been built up in the media as the film of the year. Such pictures get the super-hype, and sometimes become a cover story on one of the opinion-molding news magazines. When the long-awaited opening finally comes, they turn out, in contrast to the promotion, to be mediocre and weak. The "overdone turkey" is the opposite of a "sleeper"—everyone thinks it is going to hit big, but it does a modest business and the notices are less than extravagant. *2001* looked as if it was going to fail this way, but its great merits overcame its overpromotion, and Stanley Kubrick laughed all the way to the bank. *Catch-22*, however, may find its way into the barnyard.

A third kind of turkey is the "turkey d'estime": a film that is recognized as superior, that receives high praise, and that possesses a great deal of artistic merit. For some reason, however, it fails badly in the theatres. Such a film was Orson Welles' *Chimes at Midnight*.

Finally, there is the sort of turkey that does very big business, earns a great deal of money, and even becomes a conversation piece in certain circles. We can call this the "stuffed turkey"; it is shoddy, shabby, artless, and corrupt. Such a film is *Joe*.

Underground

(1) There is great confusion about underground films because a lot of people can't distinguish between the underground aesthetic and the underground "look." As a result, they describe anything that is badly shot, ineptly edited, has indecipherable sound, and is awkwardly performed as an "underground film," on the mistaken assumption that such crudities are accountable only for aesthetic reasons and cannot be a function of a filmmaker's amateurishness.

(2) The dilemma faced by the serious underground filmmaker is that his work is encompassed by a catch-all definition that also encompasses a lot of other kinds of films. The viewer looks at his picture, notices certain superficial aspects, and says "underground!" either to put the filmmaker down because he hates "bad" films, or to exalt him because he loves "bad" films. In other words, most people who look at underground films cannot distinguish between the bad that contains good, and the just plain bad. The serious underground filmmaker usually doesn't suffer over this because the serious underground filmmaker doesn't care if he is hated or loved. What he cannot abide is indifference, and indifference is mostly what he gets.

(3) There is about the world of underground filmmaking the mystique of the *salon des refusés*. The underground filmmaker knows that Gauguin and Van Gogh, Monet and Renoir, were all laughed at in their

time, and so he accepts the scorn of the philistines and hopes that, like these French painters of the nineteenth century, he will in due course be recognized for the master that he is. He forgets that the neglect of these painters and their subsequent recognition has paved the way for instant success in the avant-garde. Today one need only set up a camera, turn it on, and shoot an eight-hour film of a man sleeping; one suffers for two or three weeks and then is hailed as a genius. This should give pause to anyone who makes underground films and goes a full year without being recognized.

(4) The world of the underground filmmaker is very similar to the world of the filmmaker who works above the ground: much of what is produced is third-rate; the underground establishment is no less parochial and opinionated than the establishment outside; the critics on the underground papers are no less impossible than the critics who write for the mass media; the struggles and dog fights are equally brutal. The filmmaker has the same problem in both worlds: he must succeed.

(5) No reasonable person can deny that there are some underground films which are works of art, and that there are serious artists who prefer to work in the underground who are not afraid of the "real world." With this qualification, a reasonable person can go on to say that it is easier to attain success in the underground than in the "real world," and that while the underground film can be characterized in many ways, the word "shabby" is the one that most frequently comes to mind.

Unions

How can anyone feel any love for a motion-picture-production craft union whose locals have been notorious bastions of racism and sexism, and whose record in regard to minority groups is among the worst of any union in the country?

Why should a man who moves around lights and plugs in cables on a motion-picture set receive a great deal more money than a man who wires a house? Why should a man who picks up and moves things around a motion-picture set receive a great deal more money than a mover who handles irreplaceable works of art at a museum? Why should a man who drives a truck filled with motion-picture equipment receive a great deal more money than a man who drives a truck filled with beer?

Why should a few men who got into motion-picture crafts many years ago have the right to lock up their union so that young people who want to work in these crafts haven't got a chance?

For what possible reason should it be acceptable in our society that admission to a union local be restricted to the sons of its members?

On what possible basis can a union that won't admit young outsiders harass and use bully tactics against these same young people when they go out and try to make a film on their own?

Why should a man who has the talent to be a director of photography spend years apprenticing as a loader and as a focus assistant?

Why should anyone respect a union that closes itself to new blood, and at the same time tries to demolish the efforts of a more reasonable rival by telling its projectionist locals to refuse to run films that bear the rival's union seal? Don't such actions belie the union's claims that only its members are capable of instilling the technical values demanded by a paying audience?

Why should anyone who has ever worked with a crew of committed young people who love film and for whom no effort is too great, look forward to the day when he must work with an overpaid oversized crew of old men who work only for money?

Is it not a fact that the motion-picture-production craft locals did everything they could to make filmmaking more expensive at the very time when the film industry, on account of falling revenues, was in desperate need of ways to reduce production costs?

Why should anyone feel sorry that production craft local members, who lived high off the hog for years and who extracted every ounce of flesh they could get with idiotic regulations and inflated demands, are now suffering a high rate of unemployment?

Visiting the Set

Orson Welles has said that there is nothing technical a director needs to know that he cannot learn in a day. This is, of course, a vast exaggeration, but one that contains an essential truth. A few days on a set, a little reading, and most of the procedures that seem so mysterious can be understood. Learning to use these procedures with ability and confidence is, of course, something else.

Film students frequently say that they would like to serve an apprenticeship by just hanging around a set and watching a director they admire at work. Many who have done this have found the experience over-rated and tedious. A much better apprenticeship is to work on a low-budget feature film from beginning to end, in a purely menial capacity if necessary, but close enough to the center of what is going on to be able to see everything and learn from the failures as well as the successes of a group of relatively inexperienced people.

People who spend a day on the set of a major film usually come away disappointed. They say about the director: "What's so great about him? I didn't hear him say a word." The reason is that most directors do not work in the open. This doesn't mean that you can't pick up something just from watching a director move around a set, but what you are seeing is that side of directing which, although very important, cannot be studied or learned in a traditional way: the exercise of leadership. (See "Directing.")

What interests film students—how a director uses his camera and how he deals with his actors—happens either inside the director's mind or in quiet consultations to which the visitor is not privy. A director's artistic concept of his film is something of which he may never speak, and which may not be apparent until the film is completed. Unless you know what this concept is, a great deal of what he does will not mean very much to you.

The way a director molds a performance may have a great deal to do with what he has said to an actor off the set, or between set-ups, or during rehearsal, or in establishing the foundation of a performance before the production started. The consultations between the director and his cameraman, including discussions prior to shooting on lighting and style and casual conferences on the set about camera placement, are also private.

The only access into these private working relationships may be the American Film Institute's motion-picture internship program in which young filmmakers are assigned to directors and are allowed to follow an entire production from pre-shooting and preparation through editing and completion. Some of the internships have been successful and some have not. The key is in the relationship the intern is able to establish with the director. If the rapport is good, the intern can become an alter-ego and he can learn a great deal.

The casual visitor, on the other hand, does not have a relationship that entitles him to inquire about the concept or listen in on the conferences. When he visits a set where he has no function and where his status as an outsider is immediately apparent, he will be treated as an annoyance. As he trips over the cables and gets in the way of the grips, he will quickly conclude, if he is at all sensitive, that this is not the way to learn to make movies.

Youth-Oriented Films

The Graduate may not have been a turning point in the art of the cinema, but it was a turning point in the direction of the industry. The enormous financial success of this picture caused the men who rule the business to look closely at their audience, and, lo and behold, an amazing discovery was made: *a majority of the film audience was under twenty-five years old.* Thus was born the myth of "the kids."

In the offices of the major companies the cry was heard: "We got to make films for these kids!" Of course, they loathed "the kids" because they did not understand them. "What's wrong with these kids?" they asked. "They don't like Charlton Heston and Doris Day, Joan Crawford and Bob Hope. They don't like happy endings and biblical spectacles and lush music and costumes by Edith Head and films shot in studios and warmed-over Broadway musicals. They go for horse-faced actors like Dustin Hoffman and unintelligible stories about a couple of guys on motorcycles, and (God help us!) *Putney Swope.* We got to do something! We got to get some people in here who understand these kids!"

Within weeks the heads began to roll, and a new breed was hired. The "hip executive" was born.

"So-and-so is really hip," your agent tells you, expecting that you will feel grateful that your project is being considered by one of your own kind. The truth is that the so-called hip executive is the same as his square peer who got the ax. The only difference is that he wears a disguise. His wild hair, scruffy beard, poor-boy clothes, pot in the desk drawer, flamboyant gestures, and four-letter words are only the outward signs of the counter-culture. Beneath it all he is the same ambitious and striving self-seeker, speaking the language of Louis B. Mayer in the vocabulary of Abbie Hoffman. His $200,000 house is decorated with posters of Huey B. Newton. He drives a beat-up

Maserati with peace signs on the fenders. He puts you down by snorting cocaine while you must be content with grass. He uses the casting couch more often than the squares, he tells you with an ironic grin, because he is into group-sex and AC-DC.

There is nothing more insulting to the young than the "youth-oriented films" that these guys have packaged and promoted. Exploitation of the human body has always been the amusing idiosyncrasy of marginal people in the business, and skin flicks are, at least, motivated by undisguised greed. But the exploitation in films of the youth culture (rock, drugs, sexual mores, despair, alienation, campus dissent, and radical politics) is the worst kind of corruption, because it represents greed disguised as anticapitalism, pedestrian trash disguised as "telling it like it is," contempt disguised as love.

If there is one kind of picture that truly degrades the screen, it is not the artless flesh epics of Russ Meyer but the arty pornography of Marty Poll. A close look at the audience for *The Magic Garden of Stanley Sweetheart* reveals a theatre filled with middle-aged men in business suits sitting several seats apart with their hats on their laps.

Getting Straight, Wild in the Streets, The Strawberry Statement, R.P.M.—the list is endless—are repulsive and corrupt films, fantasies about subjects their makers do not understand, manufactured to rip off a huge hunk of the spending power of the young. The difference between this garbage and the few honest films about youth (such as *Greetings!, If . . .* , and *Alice's Restaurant*) does not escape the intended under-twenty-five audience: the "kids" are showing their disgust by staying away from the box-office.

One good result may be the termination of the hip

executive. But watch out! Now that *Love Story* has become the new golden hen, we can look forward to the "executive with heart": the guy with close-cropped hair and an overfed build; suits tailored to look as though they came off the rack at Sears Roebuck and a picture of Billy Graham behind the desk; the guy who likes a good old-fashioned belly laugh and a good old-fashioned cry. "No more of this youth crap," he'll tell you. "If it's good enough for my mother, it's good enough for me. There's a great audience out there in Middle America. We got to start previewing in Sun City and St. Augustine. Folks are sick of all these nude bodies and commie perversions. They like real people, people they can identify with. We got to start orienting our movies toward Agnewland."

Zoo, The

The film industry is a zoo filled with wild animals. The young filmmaker is like a yearling deer wandering around among ruthless gorillas, vicious pigs, slippery lizards, scavenger hyenas, and carrion-eating jackals. The great difference between the zoo of the film industry and a real zoo is that in the zoo of the film industry there are no cages. BEWARE THE ANIMALS. They run wild and feed on the young filmmaker. The only law here is the law of the jungle.